MW01075812

The Galilean Gene ™

Disciple by Design

by Troy Ervin

STM Publication

16851 Pine Forest Dr
White Springs, FL 32096
www.stmpublication.com

All rights reserved. No portion of this book may be
reproduced without written permission from the publisher.

Unless otherwise noted, all Scripture references are
from the King James Version
of the Bible.

HOLY BIBLE, KING JAMES VERSION © 1972, 1976,
1979,1983,
1984, 1985 Thomas Nelson Inc.

HOLY BIBLE, New King James Version © 1983, 1987,
Thomas Nelson Inc.

HOLY BIBLE, New Living Translation © 1995
Thomas Nelson Inc.

Manufactured in the United States of America

Library of Congress Cataloging-in-Publication Data
Troy Ervin

ISBN: 978-0-9789842-9-8

The Galilean Gene™ *Disciple by Design*
Copyright © 2007 by Troy Ervin

Inspirational:
1. Discipleship. 2. Spiritual Growth. 3. Christian Living.

For more books contact:
www.stmpublication.com
Or www.kingswayfellowship.org

CONTENTS

Dedication

I would like to dedicate this book to my wife, Mandy, who is my best friend; for her support while writing this book and for her daily encouragement in life and ministry.

To my children, Katie and Alex, who make me a proud father.

To my parents, Robert G. and Mary Kathryn, for their example in life and Christian heritage.

To my Pastor, A.B. Maloy, for his mentorship, friendship and encouragement.

To my family, friends and staff who helped with this manuscript to become a reality.

To the congregation of Kingsway Fellowship who has demonstrated their love, kindness and support to my family and me.

And most importantly, to Jesus Christ, who saved me and called me into His kingdom. I am eternally grateful.

Foreword

Long before we were called Christians; before anyone ever thought about being called a Baptist, Methodist, Episcopalian or Presbyterian, we were simply known as disciples. In those days, when being a disciple of Christ meant that you were in danger of losing your family, your possessions and perhaps even your life; people did not need to distinguish themselves as being spirit-filled, born again or even radically saved. In those days, when anyone willing to follow in the footsteps of the lowly Galilean was risking life and limb, being called a disciple was quite enough.

Before there were bishops and deacons; before general superintendents and district overseers; before there were college presidents and seminary graduates, there were simply disciples. Before noteworthy titles adorned the prefix of a person's name or leaders gladly displayed their certificates of achievement on the decorated walls of their offices, those who gathered in the sacred assembly of Christ were perfectly content being called a disciple.

In fact, before we were ever known as Christians, we were known as disciples.

A disciple follows somebody. A disciple is dedicated to somebody. A disciple is committed to somebody. A disciple has been radically changed and born again. The very word "disciple" comes from the root word, discipline. A disciple is a person who relishes the teachings of his or her master and tunes a deaf ear to all other voices in the world. The ancient Jews used to use a common phrase that said, "The disciple should be covered in the dust of his Rabbi." How true!

But how do we make these kinds of disciples?

Our names and titles would have meant nothing to the First Century saints. There was something in them; something that made them who they were; something that gave them the power to change the world, destroy the work of the enemy, perform miracles and love one another.

Something gave them the ability to become disciples of Jesus Christ and live together as one. They all shared a common, internal force that changed them from inside out. More than names and titles could ever do, this internal power made them children of God and disciples of our Lord Jesus Christ. They all shared the same genetic code. They had all been *born from above*. There was an internal change. This gave them an identity greater than any title or name could ever give them.

Jesus knew that names and titles could not give these world changers what they needed in order to preach the gospel to every nation. A name and a title would fail them when they would stand before kings and emperors; when they would face angry mobs; when they would stand toe-to-toe against the devil without a flinch; when they would look their executioners in eye and pray for God to forgive them. No, a simple title or a name would not give these men what they needed to succeed. Something more radical had to be done. They needed a change in their very natures; a change at the cellular level. They needed a DNA transplant that would give them the meekness of lamb with the boldness of a lion.

Today, we have many titles and much confusion about who is and who is not a true believer. We refer to everyone who celebrates Christmas and Easter as being a Christian. While as high as 80% of the people living in the United States refer to themselves as Christians, ask any pastor and they will tell you that precious few of these people ever show for worship services, volunteer for ministry or give their tithe into the treasury. Are they really covered in the dust of their Rabbi? Can we honestly believe that these people would have worn the disgrace and hardships of being called a disciple of Jesus during Biblical times? Can we honestly believe that they love the Lord with all of their heart, strength, soul and mind when they can hardly worship Him with other disciples once a week when given a free and open invitation? Have these people really been born again? Do they share the *Galilean Gene*?

The disciples of the First Century may have a hard time recognizing what has happened to the concept of being a disciple in the last two millennia.

Earnest attempts have been made to rectify this problem. Many titles have emerged over the past century to try and put some distance between those who truly follow Jesus verses those who follow in name only. Terms like Born-Again, Conservative, Fundamental, Bible-Believing, Pentecostal and Charismatic are only a few. Perhaps a lesson from history is appropriate here. How about returning to the original word used by Jesus to describe His followers- disciple! Jesus did not command the church to make Baptists, Nazarenes, Methodists, Pentecostals, etc. He commanded the church to make disciples.

The question is this: Do we even know what a true disciple looks like?

Pastor Troy Ervin is addressing one of the most vital issues facing the church today - true, Biblical discipleship. He does so by wiping away the religious facade of modern Christianity and peering at discipleship from the cellular level. He bores a hole in all the titles and talk, discovering the root of being a disciple of Christ - being born again from the seed of God. While so many people are caught up in the faddish and stylistic nuisances of how to "do church" in America to attract larger crowds, he has brought forth a manuscript that describes the core of the being a disciple!

This may be one of the most important books in your library. In it, you will find what it means to be a disciple of Jesus Christ. Get ready to lose your fascination with titles and pet names. Be ready to lose your preferred terms of identity like Catholic, Reformed, Lutheran and Independent. Be ready to lose your attraction for the things of this world and return to your first love. This book will challenge you, encourage you, teach you and may even anger you. But let it all happen. For within these pages, you will find your personal journey of discipleship and very soon you, too, will discover if you share the *Galilean Gene*!

Introduction

The main role of DNA in a cell is the long-term storage of information. DNA carries genetic information, which are called genes. The Gospels record the preeminent long-term information that unravels the spiritual DNA necessary to be a disciple and expresses the genetic code of Jesus.

Never before has a book tackled this topic in this format until now! In his book, **The Galilean Gene**: *The Characteristics of a Disciple*, Pastor Troy Ervin reveals the spiritual genetic code of Christ. *Genetics* (from the Greek, *genno* **γεννώ** = give birth) is the science of genes, heredity, and the variation of organisms. The new birth experience imparts the Spiritual genetic code of Christ and transfers the characteristics for discipleship.

The New Testament clearly describes the nature and character of Christ. Ervin carefully analyzes the spiritual significance of the believer by using a comparison contrast with the concepts of DNA, genetic coding, chromosome structuring and the hereditary traits of a gene.

It has been two-thousand years since Christ performed His miracles and shared His teaching. As each year goes by, we get farther away from the original Jesus. How does today's church present Jesus and what do they say He looked like? What kind of Jesus are we offering to our society?

Discipleship is the true reflection of Jesus. Our Lord made it clear that unless we take up our cross and follow Him we cannot be His disciple. What are the necessary qualities to be a disciple? Pastor Ervin says, they can be found in the spiritual DNA structure, call **The Galilean Gene**. In this riveting book, you will discover the genetic traits necessary to be a true disciple of Christ.

Part One:

The Genetic Code

1

———

Spiritual Genetics

The Definition

A *gene* is a hereditary unit consisting of a sequence of DNA that occupies a specific location. Genes interact with each other to influence physical development, behavior and are working subunits of DNA. DNA is a vast information database that carries the complete set of instructions for making all the proteins a cell will ever need. Each gene contains a particular set of instructions, usually a coding for a particular protein. These instructions calculate the genetic code.

Genetics is the study of how living things receive common traits from previous generations. These traits are described by the genetic information and are carried by a molecule called DNA. The instructions for constructing and operating an organism are contained in the DNA. Every living thing on earth has DNA in its cells.

Deoxyribonucleic acid (DNA) is the body's instruction manual for making you who you are. It is present in any living being. It carries all of the instructions for making the structures and materials the body needs to function. All of the cells of an individual contain the same DNA, essentially creating a specific *identity* for that individual.

A gene is a *hereditary* unit consisting of DNA that occupies a spot on a chromosome and determines a characteristic in an organism. Genes are passed on from parent to child and are believed by many to be an important determinant of looks and behavior. Scientists believe that both your environment and your genes influence the person you become. However, searching for genes involved in behavior is controversial, especially for those genes that may influence aggressive or addictive behavior.1

Behavior: Learned versus Inherited

One debate in psychology, linguistics, and other social sciences is about whether or not human behavior (animal behavior and all other kinds of behavior) is determined by genetic or environmental factors. It is a debate about what determines a very specific mode of behavior.

You need an heir to pass your kingdom. The debate is probably an ultimately fruitless one because its environment is ridiculously complex from a very early stage; genetics determine, for instance, what sorts of chemicals are released into the womb during gestation - so do we call those chemicals *innate* factors or *environmental* factors? Eventually the entire argument reduces to semantics, in the worst sense of the word. Similarly, how one looks (arguably genetic) influences how one is treated (arguably environmental), which in turn influences a number of other factors, some of which eventually affect how you look.

A friend of our family adopted a girl when she was 18 months old. She was raised in a good home and lived an average life. When she was an adult, she wanted to find her biological mother. She was able to discover her whereabouts and eventually met her. Her mother had no previous contact with her and did not see her daughter until she was 19 years old. However, this girl physically looked like her mother and after sometime, it was obvious that their interests, verbal skills and behavior were exactly alike. She was raised in a different home, but she still had her mother's genes.

There are certain features that only come from DNA. This genetic code structure will add validity and verify chemical make up. To identify the parental source a DNA test will ensure accuracy up to 99.99%. The genetic inheritance is an absolute. A person's DNA is directly linked to his or her mother and father. The bottom line, you can prove who your Daddy is.

The DNA is your *behavioral inheritance*. It is what determines who you are. The Bible says, *"But as many as received him, to them gave he power to become the sons of God, even them that believe on his name"* (John 1:12). The word power comes from the Greek word, *exousia*, which means "right or privilege".2 *Exousia* is a word that represents bequeathed or *inherited authority*. In other words, a person receives his or her legal or royal rights through inherited genetics.

In ancient Greek history, a king would bequeath his throne to his direct heir. Alexander the Great died at age 33. His wife was pregnant at the time and did not give birth until after his death. But because the child was born after his death, his kingdom was divided into four regions to four separate generals. He needed an heir to whom he could pass his kingdom.

In England, the biological family controls the rights to the throne. A son can only become a prince or king by being a direct biological successor. Prince Harry and Prince William have the legal right to carry that title because their father, Prince Charles Arthur Philip George, is the Prince of Wales in the United Kingdom. Prince Charles is first in line to the throne, William is second and Harry is third. They were not elected or appointed to their office; they inherited it through their bloodline.

This is what John meant when he said, *"To them gave he the power* (genetic inheritance) *to become the sons of God."* The *exousia* is a believer's inherited spiritual DNA. The only way to become a son or daughter of God is to inherit God's genetic code through the Holy Spirit. When we inherit God's DNA, we become royalty. It instantly makes us an heir to God.

Born of God

The idea of genetics and spiritual DNA is developed by the terminology in Johannine Literature (Writings of John). He developed this idea by using specific expressions relative to conception and birthing. God's Word tells us, *"Whosoever is born of God doth not commit sin; for his **seed** remaineth in him;*

and he cannot sin, because he is born of God" (1 John 3:9, emphasis mine). The word *seed* is the Greek word *sperma*, where we get our English word sperm. Its Old Testament equivalent counterpart is *zara*. *Zara* is the Hebrew word translated "seed".3 Genesis 3:15 says, God will put enmity between Satan and the woman, *"And between your <u>seed</u> and her <u>Seed</u>"* (NKVJ, underline emphasis is mine).

John says those who are of God receive His *seed*. *Sperma* occurs 44 times in the New Testament.4 This "divine seed" (*sperma*) carries life and the *Galilean Gene*. It signifies the divine principle of life. As the physical *sperma* was the generator of life in the physical order, so the divine *sperma* becomes the source and origin of life in the new order of recreated humanity.

Christ is called the SEED in Galatians 3:16. Paul says the He is THE only descendent of Abraham that carries the blessing. This seed (source of life) was placed inside the Virgin Mary. In similar manner, the Holy Spirit carries the blessing of Abraham and the genetic code of the Father to His children. *"Being born again, not of corruptible <u>seed</u>, but of incorruptible, by the word of God, which liveth and abideth for ever"* (1 Peter 1:23, emphasis mine).

In the natural, the DNA code comes from a father and a mother. When a sperm and egg combine, it causes a chemical fusion. This combination creates an original DNA structure that forms a new life. God Himself imparts His DNA into our spirit creating a fusion, the result—a new nature. Peter tells us that we become *"partakers of the divine nature"* (2 Peter 1:4), thus we inherit God's DNA!

God's DNA or nature transforms our previous nature. We receive a reformation of our spiritual chromosome structure and inherit a unique DNA code. Paul said it like this,

> *"That ye put off concerning the former conversation the old man, which is corrupt according to the deceitful lust; And be renewed in the spirit of your mind;*

> *And that ye put on the new man, which after God is created in righteousness and true holiness"* (Eph. 4:22-24).

The use of this Old English term "man" refers to the *spiritual nature*. The spiritual nature is what makes up an individuals spiritual identity. It is who we REALLY are! When a person receives God, he or she receives the genetic code of God. It is His nature, righteous and holiness.

John further develops this idea of genetics in John 3:3, *"Jesus answered and said unto him, Verily, verily, I say unto thee, Except a man be born again, he cannot see the kingdom of God."* This transformation is called being "born again". This word *again* is a Greek word, *ana*, which literally means "up or above". The same Greek word (ανωθεν) which is translated, "born *again"* in verse three is the exact same Greek word John uses in verse thirty-one where it is translated, *"He that cometh from* **above** (ανωθεν) *is above* [literally, 'over' επανω] *all"* (emphasis mine). Therefore, we should technically call it "born from above".

He couldn't even cuss right.

To be *born again* means to be *born from above*. It happens when an individual comes through the birth canal of God. This experience identifies an individual with the source of his or her life. Their Father is from above. The identity, DNA, genetic code is the *Galilean Gene* that comes from above!

Jesus continued His conversation with Nicodemus. *"Jesus answered, Verily, verily, I say unto thee, Except a man be born of water and of the Spirit, he cannot enter into the kingdom of God"* (John 3:6). The term water refers to the physical. In other words, a man is born physically, but a man must also be born spiritually to enter the kingdom of God. The seed of a man produces natural life; the seed of God brings spiritual life. The first brings you into the world and the second brings you into the kingdom.

DNA Identity

The new birth experience identifies us with the kingdom. To be in the kingdom we <u>must</u> be *born from above*. When we are *born from above,* we have the heavenly Father's DNA. The *Galilean Gene* is the new genetic code that reforms our behavior. At that point, we have a new nature, a new spirit, a new character, and a new hereditary structure. We will begin to look, act and live like the ONE who gave us our identity. The *Galilean Gene* will cause us to be a copycat, a duplicate of the original gene—Jesus.

This identity was in Peter. After Pentecost, Peter and John were arrested for using the name of Jesus for healing. The religious leaders were unsure what to do with them. *"Now when they saw the boldness of Peter and John, and perceived that they were unlearned and ignorant men, they marveled; and they took knowledge of them, that they had been with Jesus"* (Acts 4:13). Peter received a DNA transfer. He looked like His Master. In fact, when Peter betrayed the Lord he denied that he was one of His disciples. But his accent and demeanor could not hide his identity. He cursed like a pagan, but he was a believer trying to pretend to be a heathen. It did not fool those who were around the campfire that night. His identity was so ingrained in his genes that he "couldn't even cuss right."

We have little information about Jesus from His birth until He started His ministry. During His childhood, God protected and prepared Him for His future. He developed in many ways, *"And Jesus increased in wisdom and stature, and in favor with God and man"* (Luke 2:52). The Bible does not tell us, but I wonder if Satan really knew who Jesus was. Concealed on the backside and in the hills of Nazareth, Jesus lived a quiet, normal life as the son of a carpenter. It seems to me that if Satan knew for sure He was the Son of God, the Messiah, he would have attempted to kill Him and we would have heard about it in the Scriptures.

At age 30, Jesus was set to enter His earthly ministry. But before He stepped into His role, He was baptized. When John baptized Jesus, a voice from heaven uttered these words, *"This is my Son, in whom I am well pleased"* (Luke 3:22). This is an interesting statement. Many scholars have an opinion with what it means, so I might as well give mine. Joseph and Mary raised Jesus, but He came from another world. His DNA was there but now He was getting His *Identity*. Now, Satan knew for sure who He was.

The next event that transpired in Jesus' life was the wilderness. The Bible says, *"And immediately the spirit driveth him into the wilderness. And he was there in the wilderness forty days, tempted of Satan; and was with the wild beasts; and the angels ministered unto him"* (Mark 1:12, 13). The adversary came after Jesus and attempted to question His identity. He said; *"If you are the Son of God"* do this (Matt. 4:3). Jesus' response was a series of quotes from Deuteronomy—God's Word. However, what He was really saying was, "My Dad just told me who I am, so leave me alone!"

Jesus was the exact replica of the Father. He possessed the Divine DNA. He was questioned about the heavenly Father by Philip when he said, *"Lord, shew us the Father"* (John 14:8). Jesus replied, *"He that hath seen me hath seen the father"* (14:9). He looked like His Daddy. But it went a step further. He did not just look like Him, He also acted like Him. You see every time the Father told the Son to do something He was speaking to His Identity. He wanted to do the will of His Father. God was speaking to Him as a Son.

When I was in grade in school, I made a "C" grade average in a particular subject. When my dad saw it he said, "Troy, if that was your performance level I could accept this, but you are my son and I know what is your potential." My Dad was reminding me of something important. He was not trying to give me identity he was calling attention to who I was. He was trying to tell me, "You come from my loins."

A disciple comes from the loins of God. The DNA structure is imparted through the presence of the Holy Spirit. The Holy Spirit is the spirit of Jesus, who is the offspring of God. Therefore, whoever receives Jesus receives the same *seed* that Mary did in her womb. You actually receive the "strand" of God.

A couple that was saved under my ministry and attended my former church had a radical conversion. This couple had no church background or previous knowledge to the matters of Scripture. They immediately began to attend church regularly and were growing spiritually every day. After about two months, they came to meet with me with some questions and concerns. They told me that they did not know why but they were beginning to feel uncomfortable. You see they had two children, had been together for over five years but were never married. I was not aware that they were not married nor had I preached a sermon on the topic of the sanctity of marriage.

But something was eating away at their conscience and they could not understand why. I explained to them about the covenant of marriage from a Biblical perspective and they realized what was wrong. When they got home that night, the woman gave her boyfriend a pillow and a blanket to sleep on the couch. Needless to say, it did not take long for them to get married.

My point is, when you receive God's DNA or what I am calling the *Galilean Gene,* your nature changes. No one has to tell you how to behave, it is not learned; it is inherited. You may not understand why, but you will begin to behave like the One from whom you received your genetic code.

Your genetics determine your identity and behavior. Those negative habits and unrighteous behaviors that you learned are not from your spiritual genes, but from your learned behavior. Your character, spiritual personality and identity have a new source. It should be a natural reaction to behave like Jesus.

The purpose of this book is to reveal the characteristics of the *Galilean Gene* and expose the learned behavior traits that do not come from your spiritual DNA. Once we come to understand that we inherit God's genes, then we will comprehend what it means to be a disciple.

Becoming a disciple is simple; it is by repentance of sin and faith in God. If we do not recognize the principles of spiritual genetics, we will live below God's standard and behave in a way that is not in agreement with our true identity. It is time to stop making excuses and giving reasons why we do not act like Jesus. Then we will comprehend what John meant when he said, *"Whoever claims to live in him must walk as Jesus did"* (1 John 2:6, NIV). It is time to discover the *Galilean Gene*.

2

Behavioral Traits that Work

At the center of all behavior are certain traits that identify the nature of a person. How common it is to see a child and say something like, "He acts just like his daddy." I heard that more than once when I was growing up. I can remember when I was seven or eight years old and was in the local grocery store when someone from our community looked at me and asked, "You're an Ervin, aren't you?" There was something about my look, posture and demeanor that made me look like an Ervin. It was in my genes and I could not do anything about it. I am an Ervin.

In the previous chapter, I discussed the genetic connection. I briefly discussed the concept of behavior; is it inherited or learned? The truth is that it is both. We conduct ourselves based upon our inherited behavior and our learned behavior. The significance of the outcome is based upon whose "inherited" genes we possess and whose learned behaviors we reenact. In other words, "Who's your Daddy?"

I am not a psychologist or a psychiatrist, but over the years of ministry, I have observed people. In my experience, I have noticed four types of behavior traits that can manifest in a person: *inherited* behavior, *learned* behavior, *modeling* behavior and *mentoring* behavior.

Inherited Behavior
Inherited behavior is to receive a characteristic or quality passed on genetically. Inherited behavior is a behavior with which a person is born, an inherited "blue print". This is an

inherited disposition from ones DNA. Afterwards his behavior will be developed through the process of maturation. Therefore, the environment has some effect on behavior and only when there are methods employed in order to change an individual's nature, such as, a brain tumor or a chemical imbalance, just to name a few, will one's behavior go against his or her DNA.

In secular psychiatry, the debate to determine if sexual preference, alcoholism, or mental illness is passed through genes cannot be proven through DNA testing. Scientists say there is no link, but psychologists disagree. They may dispute this matter for years, but I can agree to this much, behavior is linked to inherited genes. The difference is whose genes we are talking about—it is dependent upon the spiritual genetic code.

Why is it so easy for all humankind to sin? You do not have to teach a baby to have a temper tantrum, to lie, steal or misbehave—it comes naturally. It is something with which he or she is born. Every person who is physically born into the world is born in sin. His or her nature is sinful. It is what some theologians call *inherited depravity*.

My daughter, Katie, is a precious girl. She is innocent, yet at the same time, she has the nature she was born with. If I caught her taking cookies out of the cookie jar and asked her if she did so, she would deny it. No one had to teach her to lie; it comes naturally based upon the sinful nature that she inherited.

This nature is inherited through Adam, the first human. The Bible says, "*Wherefore, as by one man sin entered into the world, and death by sin; and so death passed upon all men, for that all have sinned*" (Romans 5:12). Total depravity speaks of the pervasiveness of the evil in man, and in all that he does, with the impossibility on man's part to perform what is truly and spiritually good in the eyes of an all-holy God. It does not mean, however; man is utterly evil in every way and the he cannot do good things. It means he or she is incapable of acting from purely unselfish motives in order to glorify the Creator, and in his or her sinful state, he or she is unable to reconcile with the righteous ruler of the universe.

God's Word says, *"The Lord saw that the wickedness of man was great on the earth, and that every intent of the thoughts of his heart was only evil continually"* (Gen. 6:5). This concept continues in Genesis, *"For the intent of man's heart is evil from his youth"* (8:21, NASB). Scripture clearly teaches that man is sinful from his birth, in fact, from the very moment of conception (Psm. 51:5), his "heart" (inner nature) is more deceitful or insidious than anything else, desperately corrupt, and incurably sick (Jer. 17:9).

The DNA in which our chromosomes are formed comes from our parents. The spiritual DNA with which we are born comes from Adam. Our nature is bent toward evil. Adam's disobedience in the Garden of Eden changed his nature from pure to evil. When he had children, the Bible says that he passed *his* image and *his* likeness, and *not God's* to his sons (Gen 5:3).

Unfortunately, Adam's nature is a false identity. It is not who God intended or desires us to be. Without God, we will live a life absent from the internal presence of the Creator and have no hope for eternal life. The evil nature which man is born with causes him to develop habits and behavior according to the spiritual DNA code he has inherited from Adam. The longer an individual cohabitates with this nature the more likely he or she will form and develop behavior patterns that are not pleasing to God.

How we behave is dependent upon our genes.

However, there is hope. Scripture tells us that man was created in God's image and likeness (Gen. 1:26). That means that we are a spirit being and a part of us still comes from God. That tiny strand is called the image of God. It is marred but not depleted. However, it does create a void, an absence of God that causes us to have selfish cravings and a search for identity. The image of God that remains (as limited as it may be), prevents humanity from losing all hope and to be restored back to God. The image of God in humankind is what causes God to pursue humanity, to redeem him from his fallen state and remove or repair his Adamic nature.

If we can believe that man has inherited sin at conception and birth, then we must believe that righteousness is inherited at the new birth. The new birth experience recodes the spiritual DNA. God reshapes the genetic structure and redistributes its hereditary nature. The individual is restored to his or her original nature, similar to what Adam was in before he fell to sin in the garden. This nature reformation takes place when we receive the *Galilean Gene*. The Bible says, *"For as by one man's disobedience many were made sinners, so by the obedience of one shall many be made righteous"* (Romans 5:19).

The old nature is replaced with a new nature. The spiritual DNA has been reconstructed, he or she has new genes in place, and now the individual must adjust, adhere, and reconfigure his or her behavior according to the regenerated genetic code.

A man in my church (I will call him Jim) became *born from above* when he was in his fifties. One day, he came into my office to meet with me over some concerns that he had. He could not figure out what was wrong. He was acting differently and could not understand why.

God had performed a miracle in Jim's life and family. Before he became a Christian, he divorced and remarried. Jim's ex-wife came to my church and was saved. Sometime later, she invited her son (with whom she had little or no contact with up to this point) to come to church. He came and was saved. He then invited his stepbrother (Jim's stepson from his second wife) to church. His stepbrother came to church and he was saved.

Jim became concerned, alarmed, suspicious and furious thinking that his ex-wife got his son and stepson to join a cult and that they were being brainwashed! Jim came to church to rescue his sons and to see how his ex-wife convinced them to get involved in a cult.

Well, Jim found what they did (Jesus) and was saved. After a few months, he came into my office.

"Pastor," Jim said in despair, "I don't know who I am anymore. I am acting out of character. I don't know what's wrong with me preacher." I asked him what he meant by saying he was acting out of character. He proceeded to tell me that he was being kind to his ex-wife and that he did not have hateful feelings anymore. He went so far as to say, "I'm nice now, what's wrong with me?"

I wanted to laugh aloud but I refrained. "Jim," I said, "Nothing is wrong with you. You are responding to your new identity. The actions you used to perform were a result of your false identity from your previous nature." Jim's inherited nature from birth was evil. Therefore, his past behavior was developed by his former sinful nature. He thought by forgiving and being kind he was acting *out of* character when actually he was acting *in* character.

Jim did not realize that his new identity was causing him to act accordingly. He could not explain why it was happening. It was a natural response to his new spiritual DNA. He had a genetic transformation.

Individuals who operate out of the sinful nature do not know who they are. They have a false sense of identity. How we behave is dependent upon our genes.

Our real identity is destined for us. God has a plan, a "blue-print" for our life. However, it will not happen until we receive the *Galilean Gene*. The Psalmist declares that we are *"fearfully and wonderfully made"* and that our *"substance* (body), *yet being unperfect, and in thy book all my members were written, which in continuance were fashioned, when as yet there was none of them"* (Psalm 139:16, emphasis mine). In other words, when we are fashioned in the womb, God has a diagram for our life already drawn in His "books" preparing us to reach our purpose and destiny.

God said to Jeremiah, *"Before I formed thee in the belly I knew thee; and before thou comest forth out of the womb I sanctified thee, and I ordained thee a prophet unto the nations"* (1:5). Our natural DNA carries certain characteristics and abilities that are intended to blend with our spiritual DNA in order to accomplish God's design. Take for instance, both Jimmy Swaggert and Jerry Lee Lewis have the same natural abilities to sing and play the piano with unusual expertise. Jimmy has used his to glorify God while Jerry Lee Lewis has used his for personal gain and notoriety. They both have equal talents but two separate identities. What makes them different is their spiritual genetic code.

At new birth, an individual receives a DNA reformation. The old nature is transformed and the *Galilean Gene* begins to take over. A new identity is installed and behavioral traits will need to amend to its new genetic code. The struggle is not with our former *nature*, it is with our former *behavior*. Our spiritual DNA has been attuned, now our behavior must do the same.

This is what Paul meant when he said, *"And be not conformed to this world: but be ye transformed by the renewing of your mind"* (Romans 12:2). We must renew our mind from our former behavioral traits and identity. We are adjusting to the new DNA strands. The church attempts to change people from the outside in while God is trying to change them from the inside out. The church needs to help them discover their identity and then their behavior will change.

The Spirit of God expresses the characteristics of the spiritual DNA. We focus on behavior. We have our lists of "does and don'ts" that new believers are to adhere to in order to be saved. Behavior is not God's focus, the heart is. The Bible says, *"For man looketh on the outward appearance, but the Lord looketh on the heart"* (1 Sam. 16:7). The Pharisees in Jesus' day placed an emphasis on their traditions, external actions and not the intention of the heart.

Churches cannot hang rules on the wall and expect the behavior to change. Laws cannot save a person nor can they make a person righteous. If an individual steps out of line, his or her spiritual DNA will react. This is what John meant when he said, *"But the anointing which ye have received of him abideth in you, and ye need not that any man teach you; but as the same anointing teacheth you of all things, and is truth, and is no lie, and even as it hath taught you, ye shall abide in him"* (1 John 2:27).

The Apostle John is not referring to an instructor, teacher, preacher, coach, or a lecturer. He is not talking about education, Vo-Tech or distance education. He is talking about the character development of an individual that has the Holy Spirit inside of him. The Holy Spirit is the tangible presence of the *Galilean Gene*. He is the person who assists someone with the DNA adjustments. John was saying you do not need anyone to teach you because the *seed*, the spiritual DNA, or the Spirit Himself will teach you something you have never learned.

Bad theology creates bad behavior.

When a man in my church was a new babe in Christ, he came to my office to share an event that had recently transpired. He was not raised in church so he was not knowledgeable of scripture. He had a conversation with a person who was a Mormon. He did not know anything about the Mormon religion. However, in the course of his discussion, he began to feel uncomfortable. He told me that what this person shared did not set right with his spirit. Here was a new Christian who could not quote the Bible but he knew something was not right. Why? It was because the information did not align with his inherited DNA, the *Galilean Gene.*

Learned Behavior

The second type of behavioral trait is called *learned behavior.* Learned behavior is the knowledge acquired through training or experience rather than being instinctual. Tests prove that some behavior is not linked genetically but is acquired through learned behavior.

Scientists who have studied monkeys have found that child abuse appears to be a learned behavior passed on from generation to generation. The ScienCentral News explains that researchers were trying to determine if the abuse was learned or genetic.

All too often, we hear of a parent arrested for abusing his or her child. Inevitably, someone asks, "How can this be?" While the exact reasons for any human behavior are complicated, researchers now have evidence that sometimes such behavior may be passed on from one generation to the next.

Because infant abuse is found in animals as well as humans, researchers have been able to study animals like Rhesus Monkeys to see if there are lessons that can be applied to humans.

In a study published in the Proceedings of the National Academy of Sciences, Dario Maestripieri of the University of Chicago reported that the infant's "early experience" being abused seems to be how the behavior is passed on, adding, "It doesn't seem to be genetically transmitted."

He found this by swapping infants "at birth between [the] abusive and non-abusive mothers" eliminating the possibility of a genetic link between mother and any abusive traits the offspring might later show.

When the infants grew up and became mothers, Maestripieri found that, "The monkeys that had been reared by abusive mother had a high chance of becoming abusive mothers, themselves. Whereas, those that were born to abusive mothers, but were reared by non-abusive mothers did not become abusive parents."[1]

When a child is young, we realize that they are affected initially by the Adamic nature. Therefore, it is paramount to teach them morals, godly principles and a basic understanding of right versus wrong. That way, when they are older, they will find it easier to adjust when they discover the spiritual DNA transformation.

Just as there are negative behavior traits that can be learned, there are positive ones as well. It is vital for an individual to comprehend their true identity and the Galilean Gene to produce a balanced life and walk according to his or her new spiritual DNA.

This is why the Bible says to deny ourselves and to take up our cross! It is a realignment with our spiritual genetic code. The *Galilean Gene* is our barometer. Our learned behavior must reposition in order for a person to act according to His genes.

In the previous chapter, I discussed how Prince Harry and William have genetically been selected to be an heirs due to the natural inheritance. However, their bloodline makes them accessible not qualified to the throne. Prince Charles of Wales will teach his two sons the characteristics of a prince. They will attend select schools and participate in private lessons for standards, ethics and behavior classes for royalty. The may have the right genes, but do they possess the right behavior to become a king?

The church needs to teach new believers how to behave like royalty. If a genetic transformation has taken place then the learned behavior must develop. We have people who are still living out of inherited sin. Their learned behavior still lingers even after their DNA has been altered.

I have heard individuals say they come from a long line of anger—it runs in their family—they say. No actually, after they receive the *Galilean Gene* they may not realize that they are acting out their learned behavior from their previous genetic code.

The church needs to teach those who are *born from above* to embrace their new inherited structure and to cease learned behavior that is not a characteristic of Christ. The teaching a person receives reinforces what is inside them. It calls attention to their identity. In doing so, the church cannot become lax or legalistic. We cannot overlook bad behavior nor emphasize that behavior adjustments are a sign of holiness or righteousness.

Righteousness is what produces a learned behavior that is similar to the character of Christ. Jesus spent 3 ½ years telling the Twelve what it meant to be a disciple. The Beatitudes in Matthew 5 describe perfectly the character-istics of a disciple and the learned behavior traits of an individual who carries the *Galilean Gene*:

> *"Blessed are the poor in spirit: for theirs is the kingdom of heaven. 4 Blessed are they that mourn: for they shall be comforted. 5 Blessed are*

the meek: for they shall inherit the earth. 6 Blessed
are they which do hunger and thirst after
righteousness: for they shall be filled. 7 Blessed are
the merciful: for they shall obtain mercy. 8 Blessed
are the pure in heart: for they shall see God.
9 Blessed are the peacemakers: for they shall be
called the children of God. 10 Blessed are they
which are persecuted for righteousness' sake: for
theirs is the kingdom of heaven. 11 Blessed are ye,
when men shall revile you, and persecute you, and
shall say all manner of evil against you falsely,for
my sake. 12 Rejoice, and be exceeding glad: for
great is your reward in heaven: for so persecuted
they the prophets which were before you.

The Beatitudes are a word picture of the *Galilean Gene*! In these nine verses, Jesus describes Himself.

Now, if we say we <u>possess</u> the *Galilean Gene* we must <u>identify</u> ourselves with Christ. The Bible declares, *"Therefore if any man be in Christ, he is a new creature: old things are passed away; behold, all things are become new"* (2 Cor. 5:17). When we are *born from above*, we possess the same nature as Christ! Paul said, *"But ye are not in the flesh, but in the Spirit, if so be that the same Spirit of God dwell in you... But if the Spirit of him that raised up Jesus from the dead dwell in you, he that raised up Christ fro the dead shall also quicken your mortal bodies by his Spirit that dwelleth in you"* (Rom. 8:9, 11).

The Spirit of Christ replaces Adam's nature and we are no longer slaves to sin but are servants of righteousness (Rom. 6:17, 18). The old nature has been destroyed and no longer lives in our spirit chamber. *"Knowing this, that our old man is crucified with him, that the body of sin [Adam's nature] might be destroyed, that henceforth we should not serve sin"* (Rom. 6:6, Insert emphasis is mine).

Bad theology creates bad behavior. If we tell the people they have two natures: evil and good, and that the war is inside their spirit and not their learned behavior traits, we have given them no hope to correct or adjust *learned behavior*. The concept of a dual nature causes confusion and individuals will struggle with their identity. *Learned behavior* are actions that come from our previous character. Once our nature is changed, we discover new principles and methods for *learned behavior*.

I hear people say all the time, "I just can't seem to please God. I try but I'm struggling." Well, let me ask you this, "How many years have you been performing *learned behavior* in the old nature forming bad habits? In Romans 7, Paul is not describing the struggle with two natures but with learned behaviors. Paul could not make himself righteous by the law before he was converted to Christianity, nor could he win the battle with legalism in his mind.

The struggle we may have is attempting to eliminate the various learned behaviors that are contrary to the character of Christ. If we attempt to do it all at once, we will find ourselves frustrated and possibly give up thinking it is an impossible task. It would be like trying to remove items in a dark room. We will find ourselves tripping over things, grabbing too much or the wrong thing. However, if we were to go into the room with a flashlight we could remove the items in a timely manner because we could visibly see it better. An individual did not create all the learned behavior traits in one night; nor will they go away immediately.

The act of exchange from one nature to another is called sanctification. Sanctification is both an initial act and a progression. While we are in our human body and in this sinful world, we will struggle with our learned behavior because of the affects from our old nature. Our spirit is holy but our behavior may not be there yet. With His strand in us, His nature will reform us. It just takes time to learn how to develop the genetic code. The Bible says, *"Now unto him that is able to do exceeding abundantly above all that we ask or think, according to the power that worketh in us"* (Eph. 3:20). We have the power but it will take some time for it to work.

We receive a new DNA – gain a new identity – but it is a lifetime process – it will take some time to mature. Maturity is they key. My son, Alex looks cute smearing mashed potatoes all over his face now that he is one, but if he does it when his twenty it will not be funny. Depending

upon the person, this new journey maybe similar to the
infant stage - God puts it in us at once yet it takes a lifetime
to develop. The learned behavior in me is catching up with
the inherited behavior.

Modeling Behavior

The third type of behavioral trait is called *modeling behavior*.
It is the demonstration of a way of behaving to somebody,
especially a child, in order for that behavior to be imitated.
My dad came from a family that was feisty. They could be
ornery at times and easily irritated. If there was a cause,
something was about to happen. Therefore, in his early
days, my Dad was somewhat of a fighter. When I was six
years old, my Dad taught me about fighting. When I was
starting grade school, my Dad pulled me aside and said,
"Now, son, every now and again you're gonna run into a
bully. And bully's like to fight." My Dad proceeded to show
me how to protect and defend myself. Then he added this
word of wisdom, "Sometimes you need to fight and
sometimes you need to run." I never considered myself to
be a fighter, but I have been known to get
a little hot-headed in a heated basketball
game.

What they are looking for is a friend!

Everyone needs a model. Paul
said, *"Wherefore I beseech you, be ye followers
of me"* (1 Cor. 4:16). Then again he said,
*"Be ye followers of me, even as I also am of
Christ"* (1 Cor. 11:1). Paul was a tangible
model to the church at Corinth and was a representation of
the replica of Christ. Paul was letting them know that he
followed the precepts of Jesus. If they wanted to know what
it was like to be with Christ, they could watch and imitate
him.

Christ is our supreme example. Amos said it well
when he declared the Lord to be our pattern, the barometer
to measure ourselves by, *"And the LORD said unto me, Amos,
what seest thou? And I said, A plumbline. Then said the Lord,
Behold, I will set a plumbline in the midst of my people Israel: I
will not again pass by them any more"* (Amos 7:8).

A model Christ expressed in His teaching was the concept of the cross. His sacrificial act to go to Calvary qualified Him to challenge His disciples to go and do likewise. To learn our identity and discover the modeling behavior we must first understand the meaning of the cross. *"And he that taketh not his cross, and followeth after me, is not worthy of me"* (Matt. 10:38). *"Then said Jesus unto his disciples, If any man will come after me, let him deny himself, and take up his cross, and follow me"* (Matt. 16:24). Here it becomes clear from the analogy of carrying the cross that Christ is calling upon believers to sacrifice their selfish interests and daily to bear reproach, misunderstanding and shame in their service for Him, even as He did in His life and death.

It is a symbol of the believer's union with Christ and sharing in a new divine life. In Christ's death, the believer died in Him to sin and to the world-system. Now he or she are to live like Paul who writes, *"I am crucified with Christ; nevertheless I live: yet not I, but Christ liveth in me: and the life which I now live in the flesh I live by the faith of the Son of God, who loved me, and gave himself for me"* (Gal. 2:20).

The sacrificial life of a believer is demonstrated with cross and best modeled in servant hood when Jesus washed the disciple's feet recorded in John 13:3-17.

> *"Jesus knowing that the Father had given all things into his hands, and that he was come from God, and went to God; 4 He riseth from supper, and laid aside his garments; and took a towel, and girded himself. 5 After that he poureth water into a basin, and began to wash the disciples' feet, and to wipe them with the towel wherewith he was girded. 6 Then cometh he to Simon Peter: and Peter saith unto him, Lord, dost thou wash my feet? 7 Jesus answered and said unto him, What I do thou knowest not now; but thou shalt know hereafter. 8 Peter saith unto him, Thou shalt never wash my feet. Jesus answered him, If I wash thee not, thou hast no part with me. 9 Simon Peter saith unto him, Lord, not my feet only, but also my hands and my head. 10 Jesus saith to him, He that is washed*

needeth not save to wash his feet, but is clean every whit: and ye are clean, but not all. 11 For he knew who should betray him; therefore said he, Ye are not all clean. 12 So after he had washed their feet, and had taken his garments, and was set down again, he said unto them, Know ye what I have done to you? 13 Ye call me Master and Lord: and ye say well; for so I am. 14 If I then, your Lord and Master, have washed your feet; ye also ought to wash one another's feet. 15 For I have given you an example, that ye should do as I have done to you. 16 Verily, verily, I say unto you, The servant is not greater than his lord; neither he that is sent greater than he that sent him. 17 If ye know these things, happy are ye if ye do them."

Mentoring Behavior

The fourth type of behavioral trait is called *mentoring behavior.* Mentoring behavior is demonstrated when somebody, usually older and more experienced, provides advice, support, watches over and fosters the progress of a younger, less experienced person.

It is clear that Jesus modeled His life as an example for others to follow. However, Jesus did not have a five-step program or offer Discipleship 101 in the Judean hills. He took twelve men and poured three plus years into their lives and only lost one. The other eleven, plus Paul, turned the known world upside down evangelizing nearly every continent and country with the gospel of Jesus Christ.

His mentoring concept was based upon relationships. He called twelve, selected three as His inner circle (James, John, and Peter) and found one (John) who was like a little brother to Him, to whom he was assigned the responsibility of caring for the Lord's mother after His death (John 19:27). Jesus mentored them by teaching, preaching the kingdom of God and sending them out two by two:

> *"Then he called his twelve disciples together, and gave them power and authority over*

all devils, and to cure diseases. 2 And he sent them to preach the kingdom of God, and to heal the sick. 3 And he said unto them, Take nothing for your journey, neither staves, nor scrip, neither bread, neither money; neither have two coats apiece. 4 And whatsoever house ye enter into, there abide, and thence depart. 5 And whosoever will not receive you, when ye go out of that city, shake off the very dust from your feet for a testimony against them. 6 And they departed, and went through the towns, preaching the gospel, and healing every where" (Luke 9:1-6).

The church needs to take people "under her wing" and build relationships to produce disciples. (I will speak in detail about this later in the book). The church must be there to confirm their spiritual DNA identity alteration. What they are looking for is a friend!

Somehow, the church has engaged in some kind of a spiritual orphanage. No one wants to take responsibility. If people come to the altar and they miss a few Sundays, people say, "Well preacher, what are you going to do about it?" What they mean is, "I am going to go find them and discover where they have been." Without relationships, mentoring behavior will not take place.

Paul told Titus the importance of mentoring behavior and stressed its significance:

"As for you, Titus, promote the kind of living that reflects wholesome teaching.2 Teach the older men to exercise self-control, to be worthy of respect, and to live wisely. They must have sound faith and be filled with love and patience.

3 Similarly, teach the older women to live in a way that honors God. They must not slander others or be heavy drinkers. Instead, they should teach others what is good.4 These older women must train the younger women to love their husbands and their children,5 to live wisely and be pure, to work in their homes,* to do good, and to be submissive to*

their husbands. Then they will not bring shame on
the word of God.
6 In the same way, encourage the young men to live
wisely.7 And you yourself must be an example to
them by doing good works of every kind. Let
everything you do reflect the integrity and
seriousness of your teaching.8 Teach the truth so
that your teaching can't be criticized. Then those
who oppose us will be ashamed and have nothing
bad to say about us" (Titus 2:1-8, NLT)

Paul continued the mentoring behavior method with
Timothy:

"Timothy, my dear son, be strong through the
grace that God gives you in Christ Jesus.2 You have
heard me teach things that have been confirmed by
many reliable witnesses. Now teach these truths to
other trustworthy people who will be able to pass
them on to others" (2 Tim. 2:1, 2, NLT).

14 *"But you must remain faithful to the things you*
have been taught. You know they are true, for you
know you can trust those who taught you.15 You
have been taught the holy Scriptures from
childhood, and they have given you the wisdom to
receive the salvation that comes by trusting in
Christ Jesus" (2 Tim. 2:14, 15, NLT).

If you notice, each of these scripture verses
emphasized relationships. There is a pattern of spiritual
fathers and mothers building rapport with younger men and
women with the intention to mentor them into maturity.

When I was in Bible College, I was privileged to
study under qualified men. I learned valuable principles to
interpret scripture and to comprehend Biblical truths.
However, some things are caught not taught. The mentoring
behavior trait is best instilled through relationships.

While studying at school, it was common for my pastor, A.B. Maloy, to stop at the college and ask me to ride with him to the hospital in Columbus, Ohio, about a 45-mile trip. We would talk on the way and he would share principles of wisdom from his life experiences. When we arrived at the hospital, he would sometimes ask me to pray over the person we were visiting. Other times, I just watched and observed.

If he was preaching at a church or holding a revival, he would invite me to attend. He would address the congregation and then say something like this, "It is good to have one of my boys with me tonight." At times, he would ask me to sing a song or share a testimony. What he was doing was mentoring me or simply put, showing me how to do ministry.

Some things are caught not taught.

Then at other times, he would call and ask, "Where are you preaching?" I would let him know my itinerary and he would go with me when I preached. Those days were vital in my life. I was gaining wisdom beyond my years. When someone pours wise counsel into a younger minister, we are learning what to do and what not to do.

On one occasion, I was preaching away and got my words mixed up. I do not remember what I said, but it was obvious I was tongue-twisted and misspoke. Afterwards, we were riding home and A.B. said, "Now, son, over the years preaching I have caught myself getting ahead of my thoughts and got my words messed up. I have discovered the best thing to do is stop and start over." He never corrected or criticized me, just used his life as an example on how to do it better.

When I performed my first funeral, I was scared to death and did not have a clue what to do. Pastor Maloy loaned me his personal clergy book with examples of funerals to give some pointers on what to do. He was truly an example of what Paul said to the Corinth church, *"For though ye have ten thousand instructors in Christ, yet have ye not many fathers: for in Christ Jesus I have begotten you through the gospel. Wherefore I beseech you, be ye followers of me. For this cause have I sent unto you Timotheus, who is my beloved son, and faithful in the Lord, who shall bring you into remembrance of my ways which be in Christ, as I teach every where in every church"* (1 Cor. 4:15-17).

The *Galilean Gene* is an *inherited* trait, it then changes our *learned* behavior, which causes us to *model* behavior after Christ and then to present the *mentoring* behavior to others in order to confirm the genetic transformation. The DNA is there, it is time to manifest its code.

3

A Disciple's DNA

The Definition

The first question we need to answer is "What does it mean to be a disciple?" In the Bible, the word for disciple literally means to sit at one's feet. The method of sitting was an act of submission. In this context, it is a person sitting at someone's feet out of an act of compliance to one's authority, wisdom and instruction. Therefore, the concept of disciple through the eyes of the orient means, to sit under a teacher, thus the meaning carries the idea of a "pupil" or "learner." When applied to the early Christians in the New Testament, it came to mean someone who declared a personal allegiance to the teachings and person of Jesus. The life of a disciple revolved around Christ.

For many, this definition thus implies it to be an apprentice or to be in some sort of internship. However, is this what Jesus was actually trying to portray? Was His goal to institute some sort of institutionalized system that would pass His teachings down through the generations? Have we placed an inappropriate view of the scriptures to define discipleship? If discipleship is the ability to gain insights from the teaching of Jesus, then what exactly are we attempting to learn?

If we look to the scriptures as a manual, a textbook or a course description for discipleship, we can miss the principles of Jesus. Some theologians, preachers and teachers look at Scripture as a support tool. They spend years studying the Bible to substantiate a view, ideology or a certain theological concept, all the while missing the LIFE of the Word.

Please, do not misunderstand my view on the holy writings. I believe in the inspired, infallible and inherent Word of God (2 Tim. 3:16). I support the canonization of the 66 books we call the Old and New Testaments. However, the Bible is more than a book! The Gospels *reveal* Him and Pauline literature *presents* Him. However, the New Testament is more than a portrait—it is a person.

The Bible is God's Word. *"For the word of God is quick, and powerful, and sharper than any twoedged sword, piercing even to the dividing asunder of soul and spirit, and of the joints and marrow, and is a discerner of the thoughts and intents of the heart"* (Hebrews 4:12). The Word is ALIVE! Therefore, it is more than words; it is active, dynamic, breathing and living. Paul said, *"All scripture is given by inspiration of God"* (2 Tim. 3:16). The word *inspiration* is the Greek word, (θεόπνευστος) *theopneustos,* literally means, "God breathed".1 When we read His word, God is so close; it is as if you can feel His breath as He exhales each sentence.

Peter continues the concept of life and conception when he wrote, *"Knowing this first, that no prophecy of the scripture is of any private interpretation. For the prophecy came not in old time by the will of man: but holy men of God spake as they were moved by the Holy Ghost"* (2 Pet. 1:20, 21). The context is the prophetic utterance of the Scriptures, but Peter chooses to use a word that enforces the idea of a *birthing*. The Greek word Peter chose for "came" and "moved" both come from the root word, φέρω pronounced phair-ow. It means "to bear, as to produce fruit, to give birth or to carry."2 With this understanding, allow me to translate this verse, "Prophesy was not borne by the will of man at any time, but men from God spoke being borne by the Holy Spirit." Peter selected a word that carries the idea of giving birth. God's Word was produced as He placed a SEED inside the heart, mind, and emotions of each writer.

The Word of God is His SEED that corresponds with the *Galilean Gene.* John calls Jesus the WORD (John 1:1, 14). Peters calls the Word the SEED that is embedded in the heart of all believers, *"Being born again, not of corruptible seed, but of incorruptible, by the word of God which liveth and abideth for ever"* (1 Pet. 1:23). His Word is part of the spiritual DNA transformation. The *born from above* experience brings about the genetic reformation. The Holy Spirit is the fusion, which performs the DNA alteration (based upon the work of Christ). The Word is the seed-strand that connects the breath of God with our spirit. The result is the *Galilean Gene* conversion!

To be a disciple means, primarily, to receive the *Galilean Gene*! It is not a course, a class, a workbook or a seminar—it is a DNA shift. To be a disciple means we have inherited the spiritual genetics of our Master. To be a disciple means we have inherited the SEED of God and have become His child.

Therefore, as a disciple of Jesus, I am with him, by choice and by grace, learning from the Holy Spirit and His Word how to live in the kingdom of God. That means how to live within the range of God's effective will, his life flowing through mine. Another important way of putting this is to say that I am learning from Jesus to live my life as He would live life if He were I. I am not necessarily learning to do everything He did, but I am learning how to do everything I do in the manner in which He did.

Plain and simple, the cross was bloody!

My main role in life, for example, is that of a professor in what is called a "research" university. As Jesus' apprentice, then, I constantly have before me the question of how He would deal with students and colleagues in the specific connections involved in such a role. How would He design a course, and why? How would He compose a test, administer it and grade it? What would His research projects be, and why? How would He teach this course or that? So as His disciple I am not necessarily learning how to do special religious things, either as a part of "full-time service" or as a part of "part-time service." My discipleship to Jesus is within clearly definable limits, not a matter of what I do, but of how I do it. And it covers everything, "religious" or not—it is a LIFESTYLE!

The teachings of Jesus in the Gospels show talents, opportunities and us how to live the life we have been given through the time, place, family, neighbors that are ours. His words left to us in scripture provide all we need in the way of general teachings about how to conduct our particular affairs. If we only put them into practice, along the lines previously discussed, most of the problems that trouble human life would be eliminated. That is why Jesus directs His teaching in Matthew 5 through 7 toward things like murder and anger, contempt and lusting, family rejection, verbal bullying. This is real life. Though His teachings do not make a life, they intersect at every point with every life.

What it's Not

A disciple is not a believer. Let me explain. The Bible says, *"You believe that there is one God. Good! Even the demons believe that and shudder"* (James 2:19, NIV). To believe Jesus is the Son of God is not enough. According to James, demons believe in God, yet we know that they are not righteous.

For example, a person may have been raised in church (i.e., regular attendance, revivals, Sunday school, etc.) all their natural life. However, when they became an adult, they may have chosen to not adhere to their upbringing and not receive Christ through repentance. Say this person becomes a drug addict or an alcoholic. His or her lifestyle does not please God nor fit with scriptural principles and they waste their life in their addiction. Despite a person's rebellious attitude towards God, church and Christianity, he or she still have knowledge of the Creator. Proverbs says, *"Train up a child in the way he should go: and when he is old, he will not depart from it"* (22:6). Solomon was saying that the grown child may walk away from his teaching, but he or she will never forget their teaching.

Now, if this person is in a bar, getting drunk and completely intoxicated, and overhears someone speaking derogatory about Christians or saying, "There is no God," he or she may speak up and defend or refute the statement. The individual believes in God but is not a Christian. This type of a person <u>is not</u> a disciple.

The term disciple is not a title, office, or position for someone that has received a ministerial calling. Do not mistake the five-fold ministry with the term disciple. The Twelve who were called by Jesus in His earthly ministry were appointed as apostles. The term disciple, when applied to the Twelve, was an expression of their relationship with the Master. The calling to be an apostle is selective; the call to be a disciple is inclusive.

What Does a Disciple Look Like?
In chapter two, we covered the concept of the cross. I would like refer to the same text and discuss it further. *"Then said Jesus unto his disciples, If any man will come after me, <u>let him deny himself,</u> and <u>take up his cross,</u> and <u>follow me"</u>* (Matt. 10:33, emphasis mine). This verse describes what a disciple looks like. Jesus tells what three things a disciple imitates once he is faced with the decision to come after Him.

1. Denial of self.
The first indication to look like a disciple is self-denial. Charles Finney said,

> "This question presupposes the existence of appetites and propensities which call for indulgence, and then it means, obviously, that in some cases this indulgence must be refused. This is the precise point of the text--a man who will follow Christ must deny himself in the sense of denying the gratification of all appetites and propensities whenever and how far soever such gratifications are forbidden by the law of benevolence. All impulses towards self-indulgence, whether in the line of avoiding things we fear, or seeking things we love, must be denied, and ruled down by a determined will whenever indulgence is not demanded but is forbidden by the law of love. Within the limits of God's law, these constitutional appetites may be indulged; beyond those limits, they

must be denied. At whatever point they run counter to the law of love to God or love to man, they must be put down."3

As a disciple, self-denial means we lose our identity. We give up our rights and submit to the Lordship of Christ. There will be times when God will direct our path in a direction we do not want to go or do not understand. Self-denial says, "I will go where you lead me to go."

In 1 Kings 5, there is a story about a man named Naaman who had leprosy. An Israeli servant who assisted his wife told him about the prophet Elisha. She said if he were to visit Elisha, *"he would recover him of his leprosy"* (2 Kings 5:3). The story tells that the prophet refused to meet with him but sent a message that if he would dip seven times in the Jordan River, he would be cured of his disease.

Be a biblical yes-man. The Bible says, *"But Naaman was wroth, and went away, and said, Behold, I thought He will surely come out to me and stand, and call on the name of the Lord his God, and strike hishand over the place, and recover the leper. Are not Abana and Pharpar, rivers of Damascus, better than all the rivers of Israel? May I not wash in them, and be clean? So he turned and went away in a rage"* (2 Kings 5:11, 12). Naaman wanted to dip in his river because of its purity. The Jordan River was muddy. Do we think we can make the terms for wholeness?

If we cannot deny ourselves, we will struggle with the will of God. A disciple of Christ has had a DNA structural change. Therefore, our spiritual genetic code connects us to the heart of the Father. Our Galilean Gene directs us to act like Jesus. We cannot allow our previous *learned behavior* to direct our course of action. Proverbs says, *"Trust in the LORD with all thine heart; and lean not unto thine own understanding"* (3:5).

2. Death of the old life.

The second indication to look like a disciple is the death of the old life. The second key in Matthew 10:33, to *"take up his cross"* is a life of surrender. John Wesley said,

> "The *denying* ourselves and the *taking up our cross*, in the full extent of the expression, is not a thing of small concern: It is not expedient only, as are some of the circumstantials of religion; but it is absolutely, indispensably necessary, either to our becoming or continuing his disciples. It is absolutely necessary, in the very nature of the thing, to our coming after Him and following Him; insomuch that, as far as we do not practise it, we are not his disciples. If we do not continually deny ourselves, we do not learn of Him, but of other masters. If we do not take up our cross daily, we do not come after Him, but after the world, or the prince of the world, or our own fleshly mind. If we are not walking in the way of the cross, we are not following Him; we are not treading in his steps; but going back from, or at least wide of, Him."[4]

Today's church has become customer-oriented. If we can get them comfortable in the pew, maybe we can win them. Are we attempting so hard not to offend non-believers that in our endeavor to seek the lost we have diluted the gospel? Plain and simple, the cross was bloody! His death was not a pretty sight!

When we invite people to become a disciple, it is not a decision, it is a crucifixion. When I say decision, I am not saying that they do not have a choice or that free will has nothing to do with it. No, God wills everyone to be saved, but not everyone chooses eternal life. We cannot offer salvation as if it is like trying to decide if you want to ride along with your friend to the convenient store. To choose to be a disciple means you will need to die to poor *learned behavior;* such as, the appetites of the world, lustful desires, anger, pride, covetousness and idolatry. It means we decide to be a biblical yes-man!

3. Daily consecration.

The third indication to look like a disciple is daily consecration. The third key in Matthew 10:33, *"and follow me"* is life were we give glory to Him. A.W. Tozer said,

> "Almost every day of my life, I am praying that "a jubilant pining and longing for God" might come back on the evangelical churches. We don't need to have our doctrine straightened out; we're as orthodox as the Pharisees of old. But this longing for God that brings spiritual torrents and whirlwinds of seeking and self-denial-this is almost gone from our midst."[5]

Have we have resorted to psychology? Do we offer five-steps to counsel out sin? The cross is the way of consecration. The word consecration literally means, "To be set apart." The Bible says, *"You shall consecrate yourselves therefore and be holy, for I am the Lord your God"* (Leviticus 20:7, NKJV). A technical definition of consecration means that you are to set yourself apart from evil, turn to the Lord and be prepared to be used by God.

Jesus proclaimed the doctrine of consecration throughout His ministry. All that we own and all our relationships are to be consecrated to God so that they do not become idols in our lives. Nothing or nobody is to be held above our relationship with Jesus Christ. The classic example is shown in Jesus' dialog with the young rich ruler (Luke 18:18-27). This ruler asked the question, "Good Teacher, what shall I do to inherit eternal life?" Although we cannot discern his attitude from his voice, we sense a potential insincerity in his question from Jesus' response to it. Jesus' first response was to challenge his sincerity in using the word "good" to describe Him. As the Son of God, Jesus was "good." However, if the ruler thought of Him as just another teacher, he would have never called Him "good," since God alone is good. Jesus then challenged him with the Ten Commandments (actually, only five of them). The ruler had the audacity to say that he had kept them all from his youth. The ruler's response showed a problem with his attitude, since nobody has kept all the commandments "from his youth." Jesus knew from his attire and possessions that the ruler was wealthy and that this wealth was an idol that came before God. Therefore, He told the man to sell all his possessions, give the money to the poor, and follow Him. At this point, the innocent "question game" had turned deadly serious, and the ruler realized that Jesus was correct in His prescription for his life. However, the wealth was more important to the man than following Jesus, so he sadly turned away.

To be a disciple is to embrace the spiritual DNA of God. Once we inherit the *Galilean Gene*, we will begin to look like Jesus. It should be a natural transaction based upon our genetic code. To be a disciple is more than attending church, reading the Bible, or taking an on-line course from a Bible institute. It is identifying with the character of Christ and reenacting His nature on a daily basis. We *surrender* to His will, we *submit* to His direction as we *sacrifice* our lives to bring glory to His name. We cannot call ourselves a disciple until we have internalized the call to the cross, deny ourselves, follow Him and then we will manifest the *Galilean Gene*!

Part Two:

The Galilean

Pattern

4

Genetic Engineering

G *enetic engineering* is a laboratory technique used by scientists to change the DNA of living organisms. We have established that DNA is the *blueprint* for the individuality of an organism. The organism relies upon the information stored in its DNA for the management of every biochemical process. The life, growth and unique features of the organism depend on its DNA. The segments of DNA, which have been associated with specific features or functions of an organism, are called *genes*.

Molecular biologists have discovered many enzymes, which change the structure of DNA in living organisms. Some of these enzymes can cut and join strands of DNA. Using such enzymes, scientists learned to cut specific genes from DNA and to build customized DNA using these genes. They also learned about *vectors*, strands of DNA such as viruses, which can infect a cell and insert themselves into its DNA.

With this knowledge, scientists started to build vectors, which incorporated genes of their choosing and used the new vectors to insert these genes into the DNA of living organisms. Genetic engineers believe they can improve the foods we eat by doing this. For example, tomatoes are sensitive to frost. This shortens their growing season. Fish, on the other hand, survive in very cold water. Scientists identified a particular gene, which enables a flounder to resist cold, and used the technology of genetic engineering to insert this 'anti-freeze' gene into a tomato. This makes it possible to extend the growing season of the tomato.[1]

Human genetic engineering refers to the controlled modification of the *human genome* (inherited gene from its parents), which is the genetic information composed of 23 pairs of chromosomes with a total of approximately 3 billion DNA base pairs containing an estimated 20,000-25,000 genes. With the arrival of DNA research and the ability to change gene expressions, it is now possible that scientists will be able to change human capacities, whether they are physical, cognitive or emotional. Human genetic engineering is still in its infancy, however, with current research, it is restricted to animals or *gene therapy*.

Scientists say, healthy humans do not need gene therapy (genetic engineering) to survive, though some believe it may prove helpful to treat certain diseases. Special *gene modification* research has been carried out on certain types of individuals, such as, the 'bubble children' whose immune system does not protect them from bacteria and conditions that cause physical irritations. The human gene therapy is still in its experimental stages. The first clinical trial began in 1990, but as of 2006, it still is theoretically inconclusive.

There are two main types of genetic engineering. *Somatic* (Greek, *soma*, body) modifications involve adding genes to cells other than egg or sperm cells. For example, if a person had a disease caused by a defective gene, a healthy gene could be added to the affected cells to treat the disorder. The distinguishing characteristic of somatic engineering is that it is not inheritable. In other words, the new gene would NOT be passed to the recipient's offspring.

The second, *germline* engineering would change genes in eggs, sperm, or very early embryos. This type of engineering IS inheritable, meaning that the modified genes would appear not only in any children that resulted from the procedure, but in all succeeding generations. This application is by far the more consequential as it could open the door to perpetual and irreversible alteration of the human species.2

Genetic engineering is being used to produce new genetic combinations that seem to be of some value to science, medicine, agriculture or industry. However, some scientists wonder if it is possible that genetic engineering can lead into areas where researchers have not had the time to determine its long lasting results or future impact on society. When it comes to human genetic engineering, some question the moral implications of man attempting to create a perfect species and eventually play God. Are we discovering cures for diseases that can save lives or are we entering into a sci-fi lifestyle that is tampering with creation and God's providence?

I am not sure I am qualified to answer these ethical or scientific questions. However, I do know this, my Bible says God breathed into man and he became a living soul (Gen. 2:7). Then, when the Lord saw that it was not good for man to be alone (Gen. 2:18), He took a rib from Adam and made a woman (Gen. 2:22, 23) who was called Eve (Gen. 3:20). (Notice I said, Adam and Eve not Adam and Steve). God specifically instructed the first couple to be fruitful, multiply and replenish the earth (Gen. 1:28). Therefore, in my opinion the only person who has the right to do genetic engineering or gene cloning is the Creator—God All Mighty!

When we begin to control the genetic makeup, man becomes God and thereby alters the purposes, plans and prophetic significance of people. I do not believe we have the right to dictate the design structure and control the divine system God uses to create. The Bible says, *"I will praise thee; for I am fearfully and wonderfully made: marvelous are thy works; and that my soul knoweth right well"* (Psm. 139:14). My motto is, "If it ain't broke, don't fix it." God has been doing just fine long before we discovered how chromosomes work and DNA functions. Let us leave the origin of man to the Creator! If not, genetic engineering just might be the method to discombobulate the DNA of man, bring chaos and disorderly conduct.

DNA Disorder

There came a point when a large number of disciples walked away from Christ. (I will talk about the demands of discipleship in a later chapter). They decided the journey was too much for them. They became diluted in their commitment and disillusioned in their understanding, thus they walked away defying the *Galilean Gene*.

Something was missing. There was no DNA transference. They were clouded and confused, which in turn caused them to abort their mission.

Something has to take place to cause the spiritual DNA transformation not to take. Something is missing! What causes a certain number of individuals not to develop? How is it some claim to possess the *Galilean Gene* but there is an apparent disorder or malfunction in the genetic structure? God is not the cause. The answer is simple.

The Bible says,

> "*From that time many of his disciples went back, and walked no more with him. 67 Then said Jesus unto the twelve, Will ye also go away? 68 Then Simon Peter answered him, Lord, to whom shall we go? thou hast the words of eternal life. 69 And we believe and are sure that thou art that Christ, the Son of the living God.*
>
> (John 6:66-69)

Spiritual Malnutrition

In John chapter six, Jesus performed a great miracle. The Master took two fish and five loaves of bread and fed 5,000 men. Some scholars say this number does not include women and children; so, there could have been up to ten or fifteen thousand people there that day. Jesus took a limited amount of supply that a little boy had brought with him and yielded it to the Master. Jesus took them, distributed them to His disciples, and dispersed the twelve to disburse the food to the masses. Everyone ate until they were full and there were twelve baskets left over.

That evening, He left the crowd, and boarded a ship headed toward Capernaum. The next day, the assembly of people chartered boats and followed Jesus to the other side of the lake. Why did these people go after Jesus? Why were they looking for Him? What was their purpose? We could ask the same question to us. Why do we seek Jesus?

Jesus exposes their motive and the type of deliverance they sought after. They were seeking what they could get from Him NOW. The Jews were looking for a Messiah but they had conditions to his description. They were not seeking a savior to save them from their sins, but for a king who would ride in to conquest and relieve them from the oppression of Caesar and the Roman Empire. They were the elect of God but were under the tyranny and the oppression of a foreign nation who opposed Jehovah. Hundreds of zealots were trying to recruit men to fight against Rome. To some, Jesus was a zealot, but He did not agree with the purposes or manner of His contemporaries.

You cannot make Jesus fit your lifestyle— that is impossible!

The crowds went to such an extent to follow Jesus. His reputation had preceded Him. He had performed numerous miracles—blinded eyes and deaf ears were opened, the lame could walk and lepers were cleansed. But the Bible says that this crowd did not seek Him for a sign or a wonder, but because they ate the loaves and were filled. In other words, they sought Him so that He would appease their carnal appetites. They were spiritually malnourished.

They sought Christ so He could fulfill their flesh. It is a picture, a contemporary example of 'dinner on the grounds'. Feed the people and you can draw a crowd. Jesus was their man of the hour. However, did they really know who He was?

Jesus realized their motive and their perception of who they thought He was. The Bible says, *"When Jesus therefore perceived that they would come and take him by force, to make him a king, he departed again into a mountain himself alone"* (John 6:15). It is obvious from the text they did not know who He was, for it says they were going to siege Him and 'make' Him king. What they did not understand was He was already a King! He is not King by our making but by virtue of whom He is! He was king in eternity past and He will be king when the world is on fire.

It is hard for me to perceive what they were thinking when the decided to make Him king. As if they could *make* the **Maker** do what they wanted or to be what they desired. How can you create Him a king when He is the origin of everything that has been created? They wanted to manipulate Jesus and make Him king on their terms.

In today's Christendom, it is way too easy for believers to worship the wrong Jesus. Do we attempt to *make* Him what we want Him to be to fit our lifestyle, belief, or culture? Are we following Him because we want to deny ourselves, pick up our cross and be a true disciple? Or is it to gain social acceptance, ease our conscience and satisfy our longings? If preachers confront those who follow 'their' Jesus with the principles of the kingdom they get mad. How dare we present a Jesus that does not fit our standard of living? They want a Liberal Jesus, a Gay Jesus, a Lesbian Jesus, a free-living Jesus, a social drinking Jesus, or a whoring Jesus. We want a Jesus to fit our way of life. You cannot make Jesus fit your lifestyle—that is impossible!

The crowd was earthly minded. They wanted a Jesus to fit their theology, cultural mindset, meet their needs, and to solve their problems. The gospel has not been given for the good of men but to bring glory to His name. Man does not receive the benefits until the Son has been glorified. He does heal, save or deliver people for their own good but also that He would receive glory. When the disciples saw the blind man (John 9) they debated who sinned to cause his disability, his sin or his parents. Jesus answered them by saying, *"Neither hath this man sinned, nor his parents: but that the works of God should be made manifest in him"* (John 9:3).

Years ago, earlier in my ministry, there was a man who attended church regularly but had not accepted Jesus as Savior. He was diagnosed with cancer. Every Sunday he would come and get in the healing line looking for God to heal him from his dreadful disease. After several weeks, I stopped and looked at him and said, "What if you never receive your healing, what then?" He just paused, stared back at me and did not say a word. I continued, "If you died in the current state you are in you will go to a devil's hell." (I knew him well to talk like this). He repented and received Jesus that day. We need to seek the right Jesus.

In the course of conversation, Jesus attempted to divert the crowd's attention to discover the proper reason to seek Him. Three times, He told them to seek after the things of heaven and not the world (6:32; 6:35; 6:51). He wanted them to see the importance of the bread of heaven. The masses were not interested in spiritual things. They wanted their needs met and that was it. When Jesus told them to follow the bread from heaven, they inquired of *Moses' manna*. They could not look beyond temporal things. They were missing the point. Jesus was telling them that they needed to be drawn by the Father.

We cannot seek Jesus on our terms! We cannot find Jesus when we want Him. We must respond when He addresses us. For instance, if I attempted to call the President of the United States, I would call the main switchboard in Washington D.C. and speak to the operator, "Hello. My name is Troy Ervin, I'm from Cincinnati, Ohio ... you know who I am I pay taxes." She would say, "Sir, can I help you?" I would reply, "I want to speak to the President, can you connect me?" Does that not sound ridiculous? Now, it would be different if the President called me. He could do so at anytime and I would respond to his call.

Likewise, do we think we can call God at anytime? We cannot seek Him on our terms. We cannot respond according to our schedule. We must respond when He calls us! The Bible says, "He will draw all men unto Himself." We come to God when the Holy Spirit convicts us and draws us—a draw to holiness—a draw to discipleship. We must respond to Him. Do we really know what it means to follow Jesus?

Human Genetic Engineering

There are those who look at Christianity like a 7/11 convenience store. They want the flexibility to go in to get what they want and out, when they want it—it is called convenience. They look at their obligation as occasional attendance and slip a few "bucks" in the offering plate and no one should expect anymore than that. They have no understanding of commitment or the meaning of discipleship. People who demonstrate this type of behavior enter a form of religion and not a relationship. The principles of true discipleship are not self-centered. The focus is to be on God not the individual.

These types of individuals want the church to fit their schedule, demands and program. They are the first to complain if the preacher preaches too long, too loud and too candid. This type of person has a genetic disorder that causes them not to act like a disciple of Jesus.

There is none like Him.

So what causes *spiritual genetic disorders*? It is a breakdown with the spiritual genetic transformation. Something or someone has affected the spiritual DNA reconstruction causing it to malfunction. A disorder takes place when the code is affected by religious humanism—a worldview that centers on man. The breakdown comes with an emphasis on situational ethics and a lack of morals.

The genetic failure takes place when man interferes with God's design. It is when humanity attempts to alter divinity. Genetic engineering produces a manufactured gene that is spiritual humanism. Our pulpits have exchanged preachers for puppeteers. They say what people want to hear. The result is a hereditary code that prevents the *Galilean Gene* from forming correctly.

Do not misunderstand the implications and the application I am attempting to illustrate. God cannot make a mistake. God does not cause or create junk, spiritual disorders, or malfunctions. God is God and He is perfect in all His ways. There is none like Him. What I am saying is man in his attempts has created a form of religion that appears to have certain qualities from God but they are synthetic imitations. The spiritual genetic engineering is man's effort to make a way to God other than Jesus. In a crude sense, it is a tower of Babel (Gen. 11:4-6).

A spiritual DNA malfunction attempts to circumvent the oracles of God and is a premise where individuals come to *their* "God" based upon a beneficial attribute. People are coming to God on the wrong premise! A new birth experience is for what they are looking. The concept of a DNA transformation is out of the question. Instead, they want life insurance with a no payment policy.

The preaching of the cross is absent from today's church. We have a self-help mentality that is coming from today's pulpits and it is idolatry. We cannot do anything to save ourselves. It takes grace! Our altars are filled with people wanting to make a decision and not a DNA transformation. A decision puts the ball in their court. Self-help gospel puts the reins in the hands of humanity. The initiative begins with God.

Our attempts to win the lost have caused a genetic breakdown or a DNA mutation. The methodology does not matter. That is immaterial. Spiritual genetic transformation takes place in the context of true conviction! Conviction is an awareness of guilt and a firm belief that causes an individual to recognize their DNA inheritance needs to be configured with God's DNA. Conviction is absent in most churches in America. What we need to produce true discipleship is repentance. Repentance is a military term, it means to "to turn." (I will speak more on this in chapter six).

True repentance will stir revival. I am not talking about special meetings planned on a calendar with a person bringing a move of God in his or her suitcase. When revival hits holiness comes to the house of God. The Bible says, *"For the time is come that judgment must begin at the house of God: and if it first begin at us, what shall the end be of them that obey not the gospel of God?"* (1 Peter 4:17). Once revival manifests in the church then conviction will come to the community.

Spiritual humanism can manifest in legalism as well. Paul said that *"Having a form of godliness, but denying the power thereof: from such turn away"* (1 Tim. 3:5). Most spiritual dysfunction comes from legalism, which is a type of spiritual mutation (faulty spiritual genetics). Legalism is an abomination and the spiritual self-help method is idolatry. Yet our churches are deeply entrenched in both.

It is time we take a DNA test and determine what is wrong. We need to reexamine the genetic inheritance to establish the disorders that are preventing individuals from experiencing the *Galilean Gene.* Men are illegally performing spiritual experiments and religious genetic engineering to pro-create a Christian that appears to be a sacred gene but actually is manufactured DNA that did not come from God.

I am concerned that we have created religious systems and programs that are trying to clone Christians but a genetic malfunction has created mutants and churchgoers absent of the *Galilean Gene.* They are missing something— the Holy Spirit. They have a form of godliness but deny the power. Without God's DNA, we cannot have LIFE!

Jesus demands something of us if we are going to follow him. There is cost. There is a price. He has placed a high supremacy on following Him. The terms are clearly drawn. We need to heed to the warning signs of genetic malfunction before it kills a generation! There are no short cuts to God. In all of our efforts, we are still man and He is still God.

Like the concerns of modern scientists, politicians and Christians who are struggling with the moral implications of cloning or genetic engineering, believers ought to be distraught as to the spiritual implications of religious mutation in the church. We are not producing disciples. We have discombobulated religious clones imitating disciples all the while the world is crying for the *Galilean Gene.*

5

The DNA Test

What is DNA Testing?

DNA is material that governs inheritance of eye color, hair color, stature, bone density and many other human and animal traits. DNA is a long, but narrow string-like object. A one-foot long string or strand of DNA is normally packed into a space roughly equal to a cube 1/millionth of an inch on a side. This is possible only because DNA is a very thin string.

Our body's cells each contain a complete sample of our DNA. There are muscle cells, brain cells, liver cells, blood cells, sperm cells and others. Every part of the body is made up of these tiny cells and each contains a sample or complement of DNA identical to that of every other cell within a given person.

Not only does the human body rely on DNA but also so do most living things including plants, animals and bacteria. A strand of DNA is made up of tiny building blocks. These blocks are linked into a specific pattern.

The DNA pattern, or genetic code as it is called, is passed through the sperm and egg to the offspring. A single sperm cell contains about three billion bases consisting of sequential strand that follow each other in a well defined chain along the strand of DNA. Each egg cell also contains three billion bases arranged in a well-defined sequence very similar, but not identical to the sperm.

A *genealogical DNA test* examines the nucleic acids at specific locations on a person's DNA for genetic genealogy purposes. The test results are meant to have no informative medical value and do not determine specific genetic diseases or disorders; they are intended only to give genealogical information. Genealogical DNA tests generally involve comparing the results of living individuals as opposed to obtaining samples from deceased people.

The general procedure for taking a genealogical DNA test involves taking a painless cheek scraping at home and mailing the sample to a genetic genealogy laboratory for testing. Some laboratories use mouthwash or chewing gum instead of cheek swabs. Some laboratories offer to store DNA samples for ease of future testing.

A man's paternal ancestry can be traced using the DNA on his Y chromosome (Y-DNA). This is useful because the Y chromosome, like many European surnames, passes from father to son, and can be used to help study surnames. Women who wish to determine their paternal ancestry can ask their father, brother, paternal uncle, paternal grandfather, or a cousin who shares the same paternal lineage to take a test for them (i.e. any male family member who has the same surname as her father).[1]

When discussing inherited genes in contrast to learned behavior in chapter two, I asked the relative question, "Who's your Daddy?" In science, DNA testing reveals the genealogical identity and can verify the identity of a missing person, even if they have deceased. I would like to continue this quest by illustrating the spiritual parallels of DNA testing.

There is a correlation between DNA testing and identifying a disciple. I have heard people say, "We are not to judge people, just be fruit inspectors." Well, I am not sure if that is correct or not. But what I do say is there is clearly a way to identify who your Daddy is if you wish to know. If we were willing to submit to a spiritual DNA test, what would it be like and how would we discover the results? "I'm glad you asked."

The Day DNA was Altered

At Pentecost God deposited the SEED of His Spirit into 120 believers that created an opportunity not afforded to believers since the creation of Adam and Eve. Theologians and Biblical Scholars teach that Old Testament believers could not enter heaven because of their inherited DNA because of the fallen state of humanity. Adam passed down a mutated spiritual gene that carried with it—inherited depravity. Believers before Pentecost did have the *Galilean Gene*. Therefore, after they died, their spirits were sent to a holding tank, called *Paradise*. Paradise is also called *Abraham's bosom*. It was a spiritual location for the departed spirit's who lived a life of faith. The actual location is not known, but what we do know is it was in a place called *Sheol*. Sheol is a Hebrew word that refers to the "grave" or more specifically, the chamber of the dead.

Christ is beyond time!

They were sent there awaiting their freedom from the curse of death. The Bible teaches that they were not in torment like those who were sent to *Gehenna*. Gehenna is a Greek word taken from the Hebrew word *Hinnom*, which means "torment, suffering" or literally, "to burn." Both Gehenna and Paradise were in Sheol but there was a great gulf between the two separating them from its sentence. On one side were the believers and on the other, non-believers. The believers awaited their departure and could not enter heaven because the blood of animals only covered their sins. To enter heaven, they needed their sins to be removed and their nature to be altered. They were waiting for the *Galilean Gene* to replace their inherited Adamic DNA.

After Jesus died and rose from the dead, He went to heaven to present Himself to the Father. Once He sat down on the mercy seat in heaven, the DNA transfer was completed. The saints in Paradise were able to leave and go to heaven based upon the atonement of Christ and the *Galilean Gene*!

However, before Jesus left the earth during his post-resurrection appearances, He once again promised His followers that He would send the Holy Spirit. This promise was fulfilled on the day of Pentecost. (I will speak further on this topic in chapter nine, The Dominant Gene). The Holy Spirit reveals Jesus, *"He will bring me glory by revealing to you whatever he receives from me"* (John 16:14, NLT). Paul said it like this, God *"set his seal of ownership on us, and put his Spirit in our hearts as a deposit, guaranteeing what is to come"* (1 Cor. 1:22, NIV, emphasis mine). And again he said, "Now it is God who has made us for this very purpose and has given us the Spirit as a *deposit, guaranteeing what is to come"* (1 Cor. 5:5, NIV, emphasis mine).

In other words, Pentecost is the official day the DNA transformation took place. One-hundred and twenty believers who tarried in the Upper Room received the *Galilean Gene* and their genetic code from the Father. But the believers did not have the ability to pass this gene, it could only begotten by the Father.

When an individual receives Christ, he or she receives His God's DNA or what we are calling the *Galilean Gene*. Their genetic structure is no longer from Adam, but from God. Their spiritual DNA has been altered and they inherit His genetic code. Therefore, if an individual submits himself or herself to the spiritual DNA test, we can discover their genealogical inheritance. Once again, we can find out "Who's their Daddy."

Three simple factors will determine the spiritual DNA of an individual. Using a DNA simulation, I call it P, P, and P. They are three spiritual genetic tests that are used to verify a person's paternal heritage. These are three P's, which stand for *position, possession* and *pursuit*.

Position

The first test is called *position*. This is a test to check the locality of a spiritual gene. The position of the individual can tell its identity and his or her genealogical information. It is what is called the "in Christ" position test. It is found in Romans chapter six:

> *"What shall we say then? Shall we continue in sin,*
> *that grace may abound? 2 God forbid. How shall*
> *we, that are dead to sin, live any longer therein?*
> *3 Know ye not, that so many of us as were baptized*
> *into Jesus Christ were baptized into his death?*
> *4 Therefore we are buried with him by baptism into*
> *death: that like as Christ was raised up from the*

> *dead by the glory of the Father, even so we also*
> *should walk in newness of life. 5 For if we have*
> *been planted together in the likeness of his death, we*
> *shall be also in the likeness of his resurrection"*
>
> (6:1-5).

This fascinating passage of scripture reveals the locality of the individual "in Christ." Paul is not speaking of water baptism, but using the concept of baptism in reference to death. To be baptized in Christ is to be identified with His death. However, Jesus died over 2,000 years ago. So how can we share in His death? It is based upon the relativity of time.

Time as we know it has a beginning and an end. It is also called the age of *Alpha* and *Omega*. It has limitations because it is bound by time. But God is not bound to the use of time. John (in the book of Revelation) quotes Jesus saying, *"I am Alpha and Omega, the beginning and the ending, saith the Lord, which is, and which was, and which is to come, the Almighty"* (Rev. 1:11). In other words, Christ is beyond time!

Eternity is not controlled or dictated by time. Eternity is always TODAY! Therefore, when an individual enters "in Christ" he or she crosses the threshold of time and come into the realm of the spirit. The spirit realm operates on the laws of space and not time. Let me put it this way, "According to the scriptures, how long shall we be in heaven?" The answer is, "FOR EVER!" Well then, "How long is FOR EVER?" We cannot measure something that has no boundary. Therefore, I say the spiritual realm is a sphere of space and not of time. Consequently, we cannot assess it by our timeframe. Every day in heaven is TODAY!

That means what happened when Jesus died 2,000 years ago, is equivalent as if it happened today. For that reason, regardless of what year on the linear calendar we choose to receive the *Galilean Gene,* we can be identified with Christ as if it was the first day offered to humanity.

Paul's definition of sin in Romans 6 is not to be mistaken as sins (deeds or actions, which are an offense).

The Greek word Paul uses for sin in this passage is a noun. It is referring to "a state of being or a position" not an action (verb). The sin of which Paul speaks is the Adamic inherited DNA with which we are born with—the fallen nature called inherited depravity. When we are positioned "in Christ", our nature is changed! We receive the spiritual DNA transformation.

Our faith in the finished work of the cross nails our sin nature and us to the tree. We are thus identified with Christ's death. Who we were before is crucified with Him and then we inherit God's genes. Paul said it like this, *"For he hath made him to be sin for us, who knew no sin; that we might be made the righteousness of God in him"* (2 Corinthians 5:21, emphasis mine).

How can we come before a holy God and appear righteous? When we receive Christ, we inherit His DNA. When the Father looks at us, He sees Christ. We are hidden "in Him." He no longer sees our sin but sees the righteousness we inherited. Christ stands before Him but we are clothed "in Christ". His DNA reveals our identity. The covering of Christ disguises us in His blood so the Father sees us through Him.

On one occasion, when I was just a kid, I went trick-or-treating on Halloween. I am the youngest in my family and I was what is sometimes called a "late-comer". My Dad was 56 when I was born. So, I was young enough to go trick-or-treating with the grand children because I was closer to their age then my siblings. Now when we went out, it was like a herd of cattle. We were jammed into one car, sitting on top of one another, riding to our destination.

I came up with an ingenious idea to get double the amount of candy. My plan—I took several masks. I would go up to the house, collect my candy, go to the end of the lengthy line, change masks and shuffle my way back to the front to gather a second portion. (I did not tell anyone for years, because I knew my Momma would have "torn me up". That is southern Ohio for "spanking".)

Each time I went through the line, it was me hiding behind a mask. But because I was disguised, they could not tell I was the same person who had previously collected candy. My true identity was hidden. This is similar to how it is with the "in Christ" theory. Our identity is hidden "in Him."

With our new identity, we can do things that we could not normally do. We can walk into the throne room of God with confidence. The Bible says, *"Having therefore, brethren, boldness to enter into the holiest by the blood of Jesus"* (Heb. 10:19). How can I walk into the presence of a holy God? I am hid "in Christ." I am covered with the blood of Jesus not of animals. The Scriptures declare, *"For the bodies of those animals, whose blood is brought into the holy place by the high priest as an offering for sin, are burned outside of the camp. Therefore Jesus also, that he might sanctify the people through his own blood, suffered outside of the gate"* (Heb. 13:11, 12). Christ's mortal wound put our former nature to death so God could open a way for the new DNA.

By being in the right position, we test positive for the *Galilean Gene*. We are "in Christ", which verifies our genealogical roots—we are His child.

> *"Being justified freely by his grace through the redemption that is in Christ Jesus"* (Romans 3:24).
>
> *"There is therefore now no condemnation to them which are in Christ Jesus, who walk not after the flesh, but after the Spirit"* (Romans 8:1)
>
> *"But of him are ye in Christ Jesus, who of God is made unto us wisdom, and righteousness, and sanctification, and redemption"* (1 Corinthians 1:30).
>
> *"If in this life only we have hope in Christ, we are of all men most miserable"* (1 Corinthians 15:19).
>
> (Underline emphasis is mine).

Possession

The second test is called *possession*. This test is to confirm the *ownership* of a spiritual gene. The ownership of the individual can tell some ones identity and his or her genealogical data. It is what is called the "in us" possession test. It is found in Ephesians chapter three:

> *"For this cause, I bow my knees to the Father of our Lord Jesus Christ, 15 from whom every family in heaven and on earth is named, 16 that he would grant you, according to the riches of his glory, that you may be strengthened with power through his Spirit in the inward man; 17 that Christ may dwell <u>in your hearts</u> through faith; to the end that you, being rooted and grounded in love, 18 may be strengthened to comprehend with all the saints what is the breadth and length and height and depth, 19 and to know Christ's love which surpasses knowledge, that you may be filled with all the fullness of God. 20 Now to him who is able to do exceedingly abundantly above all that we ask or think, according to the power that works <u>in us</u>, 21 to him be the glory in the assembly and in Christ Jesus to all generations forever and ever. Amen."* (3:14-21).

Paul prays a spiritual blessing over the believers at Ephesus declaring their ownership with the Father through Christ. He explains how God's glory brings power. This power produces love. This love surpasses knowledge. This knowledge increases faith. With God's DNA, we cannot imagine the potential outcome of our future because it is beyond our comprehension. The FULLNESS of GOD is at work inside us!

God pursues us!

How can the fullness of God be inside us? When we have God's DNA, we possess His genes. In other words, it is not us, but Him, in us that enable us to accomplish our destiny and goals. We may appear to be insignificant or spiritual anemic, but we cannot forget who our Daddy is!

The fullness of God is expressed in our genetic code. Our actions depict His presence and His presence predicts our actions. We are inseparable by spiritual genes.

The first time I ever saw the ocean was when I was twenty-five. I grew up in a small town called Wellston and for some reason we did not travel much out of the county. So, when I had the opportunity to travel I ventured out looking to see sights I had never seen before. I always wanted to hear the oceans waves roar and to look beyond the horizon.

Wondering what it would be like to see a large body of water, I gazed out over the sea watching the sunrise like I was a child. As I stood there, I remembered my mother had never seen the ocean. So, I found a bottle and filled it fill with ocean water. When I returned to Ohio, I went to my mother's house to give her the bottle of "ocean water." I said, "Momma, when I was gazing across the waters, I realized you had never seen the ocean, so I brought it to you." I placed the bottle in front of her on the table. She paused for a moment staring at the bottle. She chuckled a bit and said, "I thought it would be bigger than that."

As humorous as it sounds, the reality was—it was the ocean—just in a bottle. If a lab tested the PH levels, it would determine that the same water that is in the ocean was in that bottle. The components of the deep-sea were enclosed in the container.

That is how it is with us. All of God is in us. The components of God's DNA are inside us. We are filled with the content of God:

> *"Blessed be the God and Father of our Lord Jesus Christ, who has <u>blessed us</u> with every spiritual blessing in the heavenly places in Christ"* (Eph. 1:3).
> *"And <u>raised us</u> up with him, and <u>made us</u> to sit with him in the heavenly places in Christ Jesus"* (Eph. 2:6).
> *"One God and Father of all, who is over all, and through all, and <u>in us</u> all"* (Eph. 4:6).
> *"To whom God would make known what is the riches of the glory of this mystery among the*

Gentiles; which is Christ in you, the hope of glory"
(Col. 1:27).

Pursuit

The third test is called *pursuit*. This test is to substantiate the *transference* of a spiritual gene. The transference of an individual can tell our identity and genealogical sequence. It is what is called the "in the chase" pursuit test. It is found in Luke chapter 19:

> *"And Jesus entered and passed through Jericho. 2 And, behold, there was a man named Zacchaeus, which was the chief among the publicans, and he was rich. 3 And he sought to see Jesus who he was; and could not for the press, because he was little of stature. 4 And he ran before, and climbed up into a sycomore tree to see him: for he was to pass that way. 5 And when Jesus came to the place, he looked up, and saw him, and said unto him, Zacchaeus, make haste, and come down; for to day I must abide at thy house. 6 And he made haste, and came down, and received him joyfully. 7 And when they saw it, they all murmured, saying, That he was gone to be guest with a man that is a sinner. 8 And Zacchaeus stood, and said unto the Lord; Behold, Lord, the half of my goods I give to the poor; and if I have taken any thing from any man by false accusation, I restore him fourfold. 9 And Jesus said unto him, This day is salvation come to this house, forsomuch as he also is a son of Abraham. 10 For the Son of man is come to seek and to save that which was lost"* (19:1-10).

When Christ pursued Zacchaeus, He called to him *"Quick, and come down! For I must be a guest in your home today"* (Luke 19:5, NLT). The chase was on! *"But the crowds were displeased, 'He has gone to be the guest of a notorious sinner,' they grumbled"* (19:7, NLT). It is in this context the Bible says, *"For the Son of man is come to seek and to save that which was lost"* (Luke 19:10). Grace knocked on Zacchaeus' house and heart. He responded to the pursuit of the Master. This is an example of the "in the chase" pursuit test. Jesus sought Zacchaeus and he responded. The drawing was to the character of Christ. He had something Zacchaeus did not and he wanted it enough to pursue the Lord. It is a two-way street. We cannot change our DNA. The transformation comes when we are *born from above*. You must be conceived of God to receive His genetic code.

We must be <u>drawn</u> to Christ. *"The Lord hath appeared of old unto me, saying, Yea, I have loved thee with an everlasting love: therefore with loving kindness have I drawn thee"* (Jer. 31:3). God is "in the chase" for humanity. Grace pursues us!

God's grace is a wonderful gift to humankind. Grace is God's love freely offered to us. We do not do anything to "earn" it. John Wesley believed that God provides us with three kinds of grace. He believed in:

1. prevenient (preparing) grace
2. accepting (justifying) grace
3. sustaining (sanctifying) grace

God's *prevenient grace* is with us from birth, preparing us for new life in Christ. "Prevenient" means "comes before." Wesley did not believe that humanity was totally "depraved" but rather God places a little spark of divine grace within us, which enables us to recognize and accept God's justifying grace. Preparing grace is "free in all for all," as Wesley used to say.

Today some call God's *justifying grace* "conversion" or being "born again." When we experience God's justifying grace, we come into that new life in Christ. Wesley believed that people have freedom of choice. We are free to accept or reject God's justifying grace. Wesley emphasized *Free Grace* saying:

> "The grace or love of God, whence cometh our salvation, is FREE IN ALL, and FREE FOR ALL.... It is free in all to whom it is given. It does not depend on any power or merit in man; no, not in any degree, neither in whole, nor in part. It does not in anywise depend either on the good

works or righteousness of the receiver; not on anything he has done, or anything he is. It does not depend on his endeavors. It does not depend on his good tempers, or good desires, or good purposes and intentions; for all these flow from the free grace of God; they are the streams only, not the fountain. They are the fruits of free grace, and not the root. They are not the cause, but the effects of it."2

Wesley believed that, after we have accepted God's grace, we are to move on in God's *sustaining grace* toward Christian perfection. Wesley believed the people could "fall from grace" or "backslide." We cannot just sit idling, claim God's salvation and then do nothing. We are to participate in what Wesley called "the means of grace" and to continue to grow in Christian life.

Some Christians tend to focus on God's justifying grace, but Wesley asserted that the Christian walk does not stop with acceptance of new life in Christ. Wesley said in his sermon, *On Repentance of Believers*:

"It is generally supposed, that repentance and faith are only the gate of religion; that they are necessary only at the beginning of our Christian course, when we are setting out in the way to the kingdom.... And this is undoubtedly true, that there is a repentance and a faith, which are, more especially, necessary at the beginning: a repentance, which is a conviction of our utter sinfulness, and guiltiness, and helplessness.... But, notwithstanding this, there is also a repentance and a faith (taking the words in another sense, a sense not quite the same, nor yet entirely different) which are requisite after we have "believed the gospel;" yea, and in every subsequent stage of our Christian course, or we cannot "run the race which is set before us." And this repentance and faith are full as necessary, in order to our *continuance* and *growth* in grace, as the former faith and repentance were, in order to our *entering* into the kingdom of God."3

God makes the first move. Grace calls us to Him. The Bible says, *"Who hath saved us, and called us with an holy calling, not according to our works, but according to his own purpose and grace, which was given us in Christ Jesus before the world began"* (2 Tim. 1:9). Charles Finney said that if God did not pursue man he would be eternally damned,

> "God, so speaks and conducts, as to commend himself to every man's conscience. The sinner's heart is entirely opposed to God; but God pursues such a course, as not to leave himself without a witness in the sinner's breast. Conscience will testify for God. Now, it is certain, that the sinner's heart must be reconciled to God, or he is eternally miserable; his judgment and conscience, will always bear witness that God is right; and unless the heart is brought over to take sides with conscience, it is self-evident that the sinner must be damned."[4]

My daughter, Katie, loves to play hide-n-seek, especially at night when it is dark. She likes to hide first. I cover my eyes and begin counting loud enough for her to hear me say, "Ready or not, here I come!" I start my pursuit for her whereabouts. It is dark so the whole time I am saying, "Where is Katie? I can't find her." Then when I do she says, "Daddy, it's your turn to hide."

The proof is in the pursuit.

She begins to count, skipping some numbers while I slither away to hide. However, it is dark. She will not be able to find me. So, I turn the light on at the staircase. Then, I turn the light on in the hallway. When I enter the bedroom, I turn on the light. Then I hide in the closet waiting for her arrival. Then I hear her shout, "Ready or not, HERE I COME!"

She begins to walk through the living room and I shout, "Katie!" I can hear her moving toward the staircase, and then I yell, "Katie?" The sound of tiny foot steps pitter-patter their way up the stairs and then stop when she reaches the top. She is standing in the upstairs hallway. I cry out again with a softer voice, "Katie?" I can hear her rush her way to the end of the hallway and pause wondering where I am hiding. Then I say again, "Katie?" She rushes into the bedroom to investigate. One more time, I whisper softly, "Katie?" She opens the door smiling from ear to ear and I bellow with glee, "Honey, you FOUND me!" And she reaches to me and I to her as we embrace with joy as only a father can with his four-year-old daughter.

Katie did the searching, but let us face, I did the finding. We do the seeking, God does the finding. Seek the Lord while He may be found. Tabernacle was all about God approaching man. Man did the work but God came to meet with them.

I could have hidden where she could not find me. In the darkness, she would have been helpless and hopeless. But I turned on the lights and then I called her name. That is how it is with God. Without Him, we are in darkness. However, the more we pursue Him, the brighter the path becomes. All the while, we seek Him, He is calling our name. Light on calls our name! In great darkness, we have seen a great light. When we reach Him He cries, "You've found me!" The truth is we could have never found Him unless He called us first. *"For he called you out of the darkness into his wonderful light"* (1 Pet. 2:9).

The Bible is clear, without Him, we are in darkness and we cannot respond to Him unless He calls us. *"Verily, verily, I say unto you, The hour is coming, and now is, when the dead shall hear the voice of the Son of God: and they that hear shall live"* (John 5:25). Once we respond to the Father's call we recognize His voice and this is the evidence needed to verify we have His DNA. *"To him the porter openeth; and the sheep <u>hear his voice</u>: and he calleth his own sheep by name, and leadeth them out. And when he putteth forth his own sheep, he goeth before them, and the sheep follow him: for they <u>know his voice</u>. And a stranger will they not follow, but will flee from him: for they know not the voice of strangers"* (John 10:3-5). The "in the chase" test proves we are His child because we know His voice. His voice is still calling to those who are lost,

"And other sheep I have, which are not of this fold: them also I must bring, and they shall <u>hear my voice</u>; and there shall be one fold, and one shepherd" (John 10:16). (Underlined emphasis is mine).

The proof is in the pursuit. *"My sheep <u>hear my voice</u>, and <u>I know them</u>, and <u>they follow me</u>"* (John 10:27, emphasis is mine). By our pursuit to His chase, we confirm our DNA. We belong to Him. We have taken the DNA test; the *position, possession,* and *pursuit* tests results are in and based upon the report, we have the *Galilean Gene.* It's final—we passed!

6

―――

A DNA Match

T hanks to the highly rated CSI series on television, many viewers are familiar with the use of DNA at crime scenes. DNA testing can assist district attorneys, private investigators and others who look to DNA for answers and evidence.

In the previous chapter, we discussed DNA testing. We discovered how it works and how to determine ones DNA. The spiritual significance is amazing. Three simple steps can determine the spiritual DNA of an individual and verify if they have the *Galilean Gene*.

A typical DNA case involves the comparison of two samples – an unknown or *evidence* sample, such as semen from a rape, and a known or *reference* sample, such as a blood sample from a suspect.

If the DNA profile obtained from the two samples are indistinguishable (they "match"), that of course is evidence for the court that the samples have a common source. But how convincing is the DNA evidence? A DNA profile consists of a combination of traits that figure to be extremely rare; therefore, the evidence is very strong that the suspect is the contributor.

DNA testing is a rather new science. But through technological advances, it has been used to convict criminals that may have never been caught and, in some cold cases, exonerated others who were innocent. In many cases, DNA testing was not available, at least not with the accuracy and expertise available today. The test can verify the identity of someone who has left a specimen at a scene of a crime or at a location in question. In addition, if the match is overwhelmingly rare, send a person to prison. However, if it does not match he cannot force it.

Test Don't Lie

Despite DNA testing, it failed to connect any members of the Duke University lacrosse team to the alleged rape of a stripper and the three boys involved were exonerated. Prosecutors dropped all charges, saying the athletes were innocent victims of a "tragic rush to accuse" by an overreaching district attorney. The prosecutor had accused the team of refusing to cooperate, calling them "a bunch of hooligans," and promised DNA evidence would finger the guilty. His case started to erode when no DNA evidence tied any player to the accuser. The North Carolina State Bar charged the prosecutor with making misleading and inflammatory comments about the athletes under suspicion. He was also charged for withholding evidence from defense attorneys and lying to the court and bar investigators.[1]

A man who spent 25 years in prison for rape was exonerated when a judge threw out his convictions because DNA evidence showed he could not have committed the attack. Jerry Miller smiled and the courtroom erupted into cheers after Cook County Circuit Court Judge, Diane Cannon, read the ruling that cleared him of all charges.

Miller, 48, had been found guilty of rape, robbery, aggravated kidnapping and aggravated battery even though he testified he was at home watching television at the time of the 1981 attack. He was paroled in March 2006, now works two jobs and lives with a family member in a Chicago suburb.[2]

A man convicted in the Miami "Bird Road Rapist" case 26 years ago was released from prison after DNA evidence from two of the five rapes of which he was accused of excluded him as the attacker.

Luis Diaz, 67, was released from prison after serving 26 years of a life sentence because of a request from prosecutors and lawyers for the Innocent Project. Judge Cristina Pereya-Shuminer vacated all five rape convictions and a life sentence against Diaz and dismissed any remaining charges against him.3

A man who spent 18 years in prison on a rape charge walked out of court a free man, exonerated by DNA evidence.

James Calvin Tillman, 44, had been imprisoned since his arrest in 1988. He was sentenced a year later to 45 years in prison. With his mother and brother by his side, a smiling Tillman talked to reporters outside the courthouse. He said he is not angry or bitter.4

Here are four of many examples that show how DNA matching can verify a person's identity. If the genetic code does not match then that individual cannot be the person who left his or her DNA at a scene of a crime. If the code does not match, you are not it.

Do You Match?

In this chapter, I want to use the illustration of DNA matching to reveal the identity of a disciple. If a person claims to be a disciple, does his or her spiritual DNA match with the *Galilean Gene*? Once the spiritual DNA test is complete, how do we match the disciple's example with the individual? In other words, what specifically identifies us with God's DNA? Do we know how we match with Jesus' genes?

Previously, I made mention of how people judge others but prefer to be called "fruit inspectors." It is not our job to investigate others. God is the judge. However, I believe it is important for individuals to judge themselves. If a person claims to be a disciple, they should be able to pass the spiritual DNA test (mentioned in the last chapter). There must be certain evidence that verifies the spiritual genes of a disciple. In this chapter, I would like to address the issue of spiritual DNA matching and discuss the evidence of a disciple.

If you were on trial for being a disciple, would there be enough DNA *evidence* to prove it without a reasonable doubt? Like natural DNA, spiritual DNA has a distinct pattern or code that can determine the Galilean Gene in a disciple. What are these determining factors? What type of evidence is necessary to convict a disciple of Christ?

Evidence that Demands a Verdict

Certain evidence used in courtrooms today can produce overwhelming results that can match a person DNA to a crime or can exonerate an individual. What type of evidence is necessary to match the spiritual DNA of a disciple with the *Galilean Gene*?

When I was a kid, we did not have a television for a long time. When we did have one, it was seldom watched. But one show I faintly remember watching was the reruns of the 1950's TV show, Perry Mason. Defense attorney Perry Mason defended dozens of falsely accused people over the course of this long-running courtroom drama, and he managed to clear every one of them of the charges against them, usually by drawing out the real criminal on the witness stand.

I am going to play the role of a Perry Mason in this chapter to illustrate the demands of discipleship. I will "cross examine" like I would in a courtroom. In other words, I am going to be "in your face". Up to this point, I have not been confrontational. However, when it came to discipleship, Jesus was very confrontational. Let us examine the evidences that demand a verdict.

1. Evidence: Focus on Jesus

John the Baptist, standing waist deep, baptizing for six months in the Jordan River, after 400 hundred years of silence had expired, caused his ministry to explode. His popularity was overwhelming. He was a voice crying in the wilderness, eating locusts and honey, preaching a wild message out in the country. After six months, thousands had come out to hear him.

Then along came Jesus, without a moments hesitation, John took the focus off of him when he declared, *"Behold the Lamb of God who takes away the sins of the world"* (John 1:29). True discipleship is not about you or me; it is all about HIM. The first evidence of a disciple is to put the focus on Jesus and not upon himself or herself.

We must lift up Jesus. It is all about Him. If we say we are full of God, but are self-consumed, and find it difficult to lift up Jesus—our spiritual gifts and all our demonstration does not prove anything. In fact, I question whether that person really knows what it means to be spirit-filled. To be self-absorbent and self-centered defies the character of the Holy Spirit. Even He, the third person of the Godhead lifts up Jesus and not Himself. He exalts and magnifies Jesus but refuses to draw attention to Himself. He is all about Jesus.

When we deny self we not only get the focus on Jesus, we do not take ownership of what does not belong to us. It is too easy to put the focus on the wrong thing—us. Preachers, if they are not careful, can take ownership of the pulpit as if it belongs to them. If the pastor has a parking spot, a private entrance and his own bathroom off his office, it does not mean the church or the ministry belongs to him.

A parishioner may enter church someday and find someone sitting in his or her seat. God forbid. What is worse is if they confront the person saying, "That's my seat." Do we actually think that we will receive more of God if we sit in the same location each Sunday?

When a church is growing with excitement and people are being saved, do we take claim to it, "It's my church?" As if, we are the only God-fearing Christians in town. If we donate the funds to purchase a 'pew' (church bench) in dedication or memory of someone and a plaque is placed on it with our name on the side, does that make it ours? Do not take me wrong, it is appropriate to acquire a row of seats, but if we have pride and act ugly toward someone who violated us by sitting in our spot, something is wrong. It is attitudes like this that indicate that something is wrong. Chances are, you do not have the *Galilean Gene*.

When I was twenty-three, I began to pastor in Columbus, Ohio. When I started, the church had about forty people and, in a matter of months (by God's power), grew to one-hundred-fifty. One day, someone sent me a letter. It was anonymous, of course. The letter went something like this, 'Pastor, I love you, and you are a great preacher.' (As a pastor, when a letter begins like this you know you are about to experience an alternate definition of love.) The letter continued, 'we are growing too fast and there are too many people.' Because it was unsigned, in my youthful and inexperienced way, I decided to respond in the pulpit.

The following Sunday morning, I took the letter with me and said with a loud voice, 'Somebody took the liberty to write me a letter to inform me of something I did not know. I exposed the contents and then declared, 'I promise you as the pastor of this church, I will do everything in my power to protect this church. I do not want to hurt anyone. I added, 'Therefore, I have decided to take care of this problem this morning.' I proceeded to stroll off the platform away from the pulpit, walked up to a fifty-year elder in the church, and showed him the letter. I called the elder by name and said, 'You have been here longer than anyone else, since there is too many we have to tell someone they are not allowed to stay. And since you have been here the longest, it seems logical to me that I start with you.' So I thanked him and his wife for being so faithful, but it was time to go. They just sat there. I asked them, 'What are you still doing here? Read the letter!' I said.

Without revelation conviction will not come.

Then I proceeded to walk to a couple and say, 'I like you and your wife, but your kids have to go. It has been nice knowing you, but they have to go.' They too just sat there dumbfounded. I asked them the same question, 'What are you still doing here? Read the letter!'

I did this several times. The congregation had mixed reactions. My logic to this illustration was that I asked good Christians to leave. If I asked the unsaved, weak or struggling Christian to leave they might not go to another church. Therefore, it is only natural to ask the stronger ones to leave. My point is, whom do we tell they can no longer remain and for what reason do I give that they must go? It was all about the letter. The letter was an indicator that we have attempted to take ownership of the church and not put the focus on Jesus.

The church belongs to God. It is not about us, but it is about winning souls and propagating the gospel. Have we attempted to take ownership of something that does not belong to us? If so, there is no evidence that we have the *Galilean Gene*.

Jesus said, *"He that findeth his life shall lose it: and he that loseth his life for my sake shall find it"* (Matt. 10:39). When you deny self, you proudly stand next to Jesus for the same cause. Jesus also said, *"For whosoever shall be ashamed of me and of my words, of him shall the Son of man be ashamed, when he shall come in his own glory, and in his Father's, and of the holy angels"* (Luke 9:26). Do we easily give up when the pressure is on or when other influences distract us? If we want the world to accept us we will eventually find out, they will not. Are we ashamed of our church, afraid to invite anyone for fear someone will break out with enthusiasm and begin to run, jump, shout or even worse, fall out on the floor? Are we ashamed of the glory?

The question is, "Are we a church attendee or a disciple?" We must take up our cross, deny ourselves and follow Him. We must die to self, die to our possessions, die to our ministry or church and crucify the flesh. Our response must be to submit to His will and take up our cross. If this is our stand, we have a DNA match.

2. Evidence: Conviction
It also takes conviction to prove we are a disciple. Conviction in a disciple manifests when he or she take a stand even when everyone else holds a different opinion. It takes conviction to determine your spiritual DNA. Here is an example of conviction:

"And it came to pass, as he was alone praying, his disciples were with him: and he asked them, saying, Whom say the people that I am? 19 They answering said, John the Baptist; but some say, Elias; and others say, that one of the old prophets is risen again. 20 He said unto them, But whom say ye that I am? Peter answering said, The Christ of God" (Luke 9:18-20).

What Peter said was out of a deep conviction. He received the information through divine revelation, for Matthew's gospel says, *"Flesh and blood hath not revealed this to you but...my father in heaven."* Some can sit in church their whole lives and never know that Jesus is the Christ unless the Holy Spirit illuminates it to them. Without revelation conviction will not come.

My sister-in-law told me about her cousin, who sat on the same church pew with her all their lives. Then recently, her cousin heard about John 3:16 and she did not know what it meant. How can this be? If we know that Jesus is the Christ, we ought to be humbled that God in His sovereignty stopped you in your tracks and He called your name.

It takes revelation and it starts with God. I have seen it all my life, people go to church for years and it seems like they will never be saved. Then all of a sudden, they become *born from above*. The Galilean Gene transforms their life. But if they want to be a disciple, there should be a deep conviction that bears evidence who they are.

One of the reasons why sinners are not being saved is because the church no longer has any conviction. We send a confusing message when national TV preachers proclaim they are not sure if Jesus is the only way to heaven or not. They have no conviction. Sinners are not going to be convicted until we are - once the church has a deep conviction that Jesus is the ONLY WAY, without apology or compromise, then the Holy Spirit will convict individuals of there sin and they will receive the genetic transfer.

Jesus is the Christ and we must have a deep conviction in our hearts. Without conviction, we will not have any convictions. I grew up in the holiness tradition. At times, they went a little too far with their views, and they tried to push their convictions off on everyone. Maybe they were not all bad. They may have gone a little overboard in some areas, but I believe they had something worth looking at. But today, we have gone the other way! We can hardly tell the difference between a Christian and a non-Christian. Do we have any convictions in the church worth keeping? Do we think we can go anywhere we want, wear whatever we want, look at whatever we want, have any kind of attitude we want, talk any way we want, be what ever we want to be and still go to heaven? I think not!

What we need in this last day is a revival of conviction. Conviction that says He is the Christ and I am willing to die for that. Are we willing to go against the grain, suffer ridicule, and persecution? If so, we have a DNA match.

3. Evidence: Confession

The third piece of evidence is *confession*. It is a formal declaration of a person's belief such as love, loyalty or faith. *"Jesus asked his disciples, saying, Whom do men say that I the Son of man am? And they said, Some say that thou art John the Baptist: some, Elias; and others, Jeremias, or one of the prophets"* (Matt. 16:13b-14). Then He emphasized His point when He said, "Who do YOU say I am?" He was asking them directly what they though of him. In this context, let me ask this, who is Jesus to us?

I like Peter's response; he steps up from the crowd, and says, "Thou art the Christ!" I agree with Peter, Jesus is the Christ, the Anointed One, the Incarnate God; He is a man and God. He died on a cross. He rose from the dead. He is coming back!

We must confess He is the Son of God. Paul said in Romans, if we confess with our mouth and believe in our heart that Jesus is Lord, we can be saved. Peter said, *"Thou*

art the Christ, the son of the living God." I believe that!
Confession is evidence of a disciple.

DNA evidence is that they will always take the
attention off from themselves and put on Jesus. John has
thousands come to him. As soon as Jesus comes forward, he
transfers the *focus* over to Jesus. John was
Jesus put   filled at birth, he had the gene. It was
natural for him to focus humbly on Jesus.

a   Christ asked His followers if they
premium   had heard what others where saying about
Him. He was checking to see if outsiders
on people. recognized His DNA. Did they know who
He was? Could they match Jesus with His
Father? The crowds were confused. They could not tell that
the *Galilean Gene* was in Jesus. They mistakenly viewed His
identity with the likings of a prophet and not with God.

3. Evidence: Consecration

Jesus said, *"If any man will come after me."* That sounds like
repentance and denial. Now we make *decisions* for Jesus. We
are afraid to tell people the need to be saved. It is more than
a decision. It is a change of life. You have to be willing to
repent. Come after me means that if I go after Him, I have
to stop going after what I am going after right now. Many
Christians pursue Jesus on Sundays, but on Mondays, they
are pursuing something different.

We need to make up our minds. We need to decide
that we are done with this world, sin, selfishness and
gossiping. Turn your back on darkness and turn to the
light—no turning back. Repent is the message of the Bible.
Every great prophet declared the message of repentance.
John the Baptist exploded on the scene like a flaming
meteorite, his message was simple, "Repent!" Jesus said the
same thing, "Repent, for the kingdom of heaven is at hand."

We have watered down the gospel and attempt to
make it simple, like the ABC's and leave out repentance. Do
we think we can hold on to our old lives, be saved and wait
until we get sanctified or spirit-filled to take care of things?
That is not the answer.

But do we over emphasize the concept of a second work of grace, baptism of the Spirit, or what ever we want to call it, and say we will quit sinning when we get further along in our walk with Christ? The truth is, you will never quit sinning until you decide to get sanctified. You must decide to turn from unrighteousness, blackness, darkness and then repent.

4. Evidence: Repentance

Repentance is more than tears. I have seen people come to the altar, cry, bawl, get very dramatic, and then go out after church and act as if they have never changed. Many times, they do not last a week. Is it possible that we look at the emotional experience as a sign of repentance? Some attempt to use Jesus as if He is our psychologist. We have our weekly meeting, we go to the altar as if it is the counselor's couch, and have Him make us feel better about everything we are doing wrong. Someone has lived like hell all week and feel bad about it so, then go to tell the counselor, Jesus, hoping to be told they are "just" human.

Repentance is more saying, "I am sorry." It is a change. Stop chasing what you were before you found Jesus. In order for the Galilean Gene to be evident, we must have a retentive spirit.

Repentance is self-denial. Jesus said, "Deny yourself." But what is our response? If we drop our nets, run through the water toward Him, then we are denying ourselves. When we deny ourselves, we put the focus on the right person and show evidence of repentance.

The church has become a marketing institution. The preacher is no longer a prophet. he is a salesmen. His new found purpose it to please the "customer" (churchgoer). He will do whatever he can do to get them in the door and sell something with the attempt to get our money. He is not a preacher, a prophet, or a man of God, he is a hireling. He is more concerned about his pulpit and his pocket book that the kingdom of God.

Now I must admit, before I was in ministry, I thought I would make a good salesman. My wife has told me that I could sell a ketchup-popsicle-stick to a woman in white gloves and a white dress. Since I have become a preacher, some have tried to convince me that my role of sharing the gospel is comparable to salesperson; thus, I am selling the gospel. No, I am not a sales representative. I did not know the gospel was for sale. That is Americanizing the gospel. My job is to preach the Bible! What those do with it after that is there choice. I cannot convince them of anything.

I am concerned that we have watered down the gospel. Churches who present the gospel with a non-confrontational, non-offensive message cannot present an offensive cross. Are preachers too afraid to confront people with the truth for fear they will offend them? This was not Jesus method, especially when it came to the young rich ruler.

People want to be pleased. The temptation is to appease their desires instead of presenting the truth. Have we lost the model of repentance? Are we allowing people to make excuses for their behavior? It is time we manifest the *Galilean Gene* and have a heart of repentance. When we do this we have a DNA match.

5. Evidence: Compassion

Another evidence of a disciple is to reflect the heart of Christ. Its basis is love. (I will speak about Love in chapter seven, the Prominent Gene.) Jesus looked at the masses with compassion.

"*And Jesus went about all the cities and villages, teaching in their synagogues, and preaching the gospel of the kingdom, and healing every sickness and every disease among the people. 36 But when he saw the multitudes, he was moved with compassion on them, because they fainted, and were scattered abroad, as sheep having no shepherd. 37 Then saith he unto his disciples, The harvest truly is plenteous, but the labourers are few; 38 Pray ye therefore the Lord of the harvest, that he*

will send forth labourers into his harvest" Matt.
9:35-38).

Jesus put a premium on people. He reached a hand
out to humanity. He was not self-centered or self-absorbed.
Do today's churches screen their attendees to determine
which ones are best fit for their church? Too many times, I
have heard people call individuals with challenges "granola
Christians", they possess "fruits, flakes or nuts." Can you
see Jesus telling the Twelve; "Do not take in Christians
who have dysfunction, baggage, issues or difficulties? They
are too high maintenance." I do not think so.

No, Jesus had compassion upon the masses. The
Greek word *compassion* is the same word in Acts 1:18,
where it describes Judas death and says, "Judas' *intestines
spilled out*." When Matthew says Jesus had compassion, he
literally was saying, Jesus *stomach turned upside down to the
point of illness* because the masses had no direction. How do
we react when we see the lost? Do we feel ill because they
have no direction, church or are without God? Or do we
feel ill because they have showed up on our doorstep and
their kids will put dirty finger marks on the walls in the
bathroom? What have we come to?

We have enough show case driven churches in
America. If a church begins to grow, those who have a
prominent position get nervous. If the church doubles or
triples in size, they begin to feel threatened. They fear
someone will join the church and take their title or place.
The growth has an adverse effect upon "outsiders." If this is
the case, we are not demonstrating compassion, but rather
coldness.

The evidence is in. Do we match the genetic code
reflecting a focus on Jesus, conviction, confession,
conviction, repentance and compassion? If so, we have a
DNA match. The *Galilean Gene* is in us. The verdict is in,
God's DNA has been found in the disciple.

Part Three:

Genes that

Fit

7

The Prominent Gene

I n genetic testing, scientists and researchers have studied the clusters of genes in animals and in various organs in humans to study protein and determine the effects of prominent genes. Studies reveal certain genes are distinguished and eminent. Prominent genes carry distinct and relevant coding that affect an organ or a certain body element. The Placenta carries prominent genes that carry protein to an unborn infant.

What does a *Prominent Gene* have to do with our relationship with God? A prominent gene is that part of our spiritual DNA that identifies is the prevailing behavior based upon the principal of God's DNA. The genetic structure of a prominent gene carries the greatest significance. To be a disciple of Christ we must carry His prominent gene.

When others look at us, do they notice the prominent *Galilean Gene*? If not, how will they know we carry His genetic code? What was Jesus' prominent gene? It is the *love gene*. The Bible says when Jesus left heaven to become a man on earth *"thought it not robbery to be equal with God: But made himself of no reputation, and took upon him the form of a servant, and was made in the likeness of men"* (Phil. 2:6, 7). Jesus did not reconsider the sacrifice He was going to have to make to become a human. The New Living Translation puts it this way, *"Though he was God, he did not demand and cling to his rights as God. He made himself nothing*; he took the humble position of a slave and appeared in human form.*"* The NLT has a footnote for *nothing*. The alternate translation is *"He laid aside his mighty power and glory."*

Before Jesus came to the earth, He was God (John 1:1). When He came to the earth, He was God (John 1:14). He was 100% God and 100% man. However, Jesus became submissive to the Father's plan and chose not to use His divine attributes while He was inside His earth suit.

Attributes are the particular qualities that describe the character of God. There are three types of attributes used to illustrate God, *moral* attributes, *absolute* attributes and *relative* attributes. Moral attributes make up the nature of God; God is holy, love, and truth. Absolute attributes make the essence of God; God is a spirit, eternal and changeless. Relative attributes the applicability of God; God is omnipresent, omnipotent and omniscient. The first two types, moral and absolute attributes, remained active in the life of Jesus while He was on earth. However, the third type, relative attributes, was not active in Jesus' life or ministry.

Therefore, Jesus could not be at multiple locations at one time. He did not use His power for His own purposes. Nor did He use His ability to access all knowledge or information for His advantage. Our Lord possessed these attributes, but He chose to not to use them. Instead, Jesus and the Father cooperated to fulfill God's will. The Scriptures say, *"I and my Father are one"* (John 10:30). This relationship caused Jesus to surrender His relative attributes and rely upon His Father's directives. The Holy Spirit revealed information to Jesus when the Father gave the command. *"For I have not spoken of myself; but the Father which sent me, he gave me a commandment, what I should say, and what I should speak"* (John 12:49).

The humility and humanity of Jesus is the divine expression of love. The *Galilean Gene* has a particular quality and it expresses itself in action—love. Love is the prominent gene. The expression of love is the quality of Christ that He said would demonstrate discipleship.

> *"A new commandment I give unto you, That ye love one another; as I have loved you, that ye also love one another. 35 By this shall all men know that ye are my disciples, if ye have love one to another."*

(John 13:34, 35)

The expression of God's love was a new commandment. Why was it NEW? God had commanded His people to love Him. Moses made it plain in the Ten Commandments. Love God. Jehovah had commanded His people to love themselves and show compassion. Leviticus 19:18 commanded Israel to love their neighbor. However, this was something different. Jesus instructed them to love their others like God. It was new because they could not love others like the Father without the *Galilean Gene*. Humanity cannot love others without His DNA—it is impossible. They had to have God in them to love others they way Jesus did.

The disciples of Christ had to recognize the prominent gene because it was so evident in Christ. So how will others know we are His disciples? The prominent gene—love—will be evident. Jesus told the attorney who questioned Him concerning the commandments to love God. And the Good Samaritan lesson is a story of love and to reach out to others.

But Jesus was telling them to love like He loved them. How did Jesus love His disciples? Jesus loved Judas despite the fact He knew he would betray Him. Jesus loved Peter despite the fact He knew he would deny Him. Jesus loved the other disciples despite the fact He knew they would run for their lives and hide when He was arrested in Gethsemane.

How does Jesus love us? The Bible says, *"But God commendedeth his love toward us, in that, while we were yet sinners, Christ died for us"* (Romans 5:8). How is it that God could reach out to me when I did not care about Him, when I did not deserve it and was deep in sin? It reminds me of the old hymn written by James Rowe, Love Lifted Me:

> I was sinking deep in sin, far from the peaceful shore,
> Very deeply stained within, sinking to rise no more,
> But the Master of the sea, heard my despairing cry,
> From the waters lifted me, now safe am I.

Love lifted me! Love lifted me!
When nothing else could help,
Love lifted me!

God reaches down to rescue us even when we were strained from God. Man is born dead (spiritually separated) from God. It is not that he does not have a spirit. It is rather that his spirit is alive to Satan and dead to, separated from, God. When Adam ate of the tree of the knowledge of good and evil, he died that day spiritually (Gen. 2:16-17) as did all of future mankind (1 Cor. 15:22a; Rom. 5:12). Comedian and filmmaker, Woody Allen, once said, "I am not afraid to die. I just don't want to be there when it happens." Well, the biblical truth of the matter is that we were there, in Adam, when death came in and death spread to A-L-L men. Herein lays man's greatest need...the solution to death. Man has a much bigger problem than just sin. He has a "consequences of sin" problem (Rom. 6:23)...he is spiritually dead!

It is a love that describes discipleship.

The love of God is a unique, proprietary love. It is a love that has only One source...God Himself. You see there is nothing more powerful than love. The love of God, in fact, is relentless. The English poet, Francis Thompson described God's love in his poem, "The Hound of Heaven." "His love is a love that never stops pursuing and giving, pursuing and giving until the object of His love... "y-o-u"... is loved into submission!"

The Greek language has four words to describe our English word "love". The first one is *eros*. The Greeks used it to express the love between man and woman, which embraces longing, craving and desire. They had a distinct interest in art and expressed it through statues. Their delight in bodily beauty and sensual desires went much deeper generating a desire for bodily ecstasy. *Eros* is the root word for erotic. It is a strong passion, which desires to have or take possession.

The second word is phileo. It is the most general word for love or regard with affection. Several words derive from *phileo*, i.e., *philos*, a friend; philema, a kiss; and compound words, such as *philosphia*, love of knowledge—philosophy.

The third word, *stergo* is used less frequently and means to love, feel affection, especially of the mutual love of parents and children.

The fourth word, *agape* in classical Greek originally meant to show honor. The New Testament uses *agape* to speak of the love of God or the way of life based on it.[1] The word agape is what Jesus was using when He told them to love as He loved. It is a selfless sacrificial love willing to give without any guarantee of a response. It is a willingness to give to someone even if they reject it. It is a love that describes discipleship.

How do we express this love? It can be demonstrated at a *time of loss*. Whether it is a loss of a loved one, a job, money, or health, agape-love must reach out to them. When they are desperate, depressed, destitute, down, in the valley it is a time to love. They need someone to walk beside them in their mourning, in the dark hour when they are hurting. To do this we will have to set time aside to pour love into their lives.

Love can be demonstrated when someone is in a *time of blessing*. We need to rejoice when someone else receives something from God. If they receive a promotion, a raise, a new car we ought to celebrate what God has done. It is too easy to be caught up with jealousy, covetousness, or murmuring over their well fortune. We must thank God that He has seen fit to bless them.

This love expresses itself when we can *reprove* and *restore people*. What is it that causes us to demand justice if we see a believer stumble or fall? (Is if we have never had a struggle). Too often believers want to be judge and jury before they even know what really happened. How did Jesus respond to those caught in sin? If we are a true disciple of Jesus, we will carry out our actions as if we have

His genes. If we carry His spiritual DNA then we will carry the wounded, not leave them for dead. In the natural, the military have a code of honor, "No one left behind."

Do we attempt to be a solution to problem or a problem to prevent a solution? How often has the local church "prayer chain" turned into a gospel-gossip line discussing other people's business? Or a simple discussion in a church hallway begins, "Oh, have your heard? I am not supposed to say anything, but they do need our prayers. Then the chase is on. The rumor-ville trail begins.

Paul said, *"Brethren, if a man be overtaken in a fault, ye which are spiritual, restore such an one in the spirit of meekness; considering thyself, lest thou also be tempted"* (Galatians 6:1). When Paul referred to a fault, he was not talking about a mistaken. The Greek word is *paraptoma*, which refers to a trespass or a sin.2 We need to take Jesus serious when He said, *"By this shall all men know that ye are my disciples."* Too often, we forget that God is able to see and hear how we respond to others.

When I say we need to take it serious, I mean it is time for us to get real about love. This is why people in the church are not delivered. Let's get real about this—the truth is, people sin. In fact, even Christians are subject to fall or sin. It is not our job to be God's uncovered agents or spiritual private investigators looking into the lives of individuals to discover what they are doing wrong. If we hear someone is doing something immoral, should we follow them with a camera or wrap our arms around them and pray for them?

What does the Bible say? *"Confess your faults (paraptoma) one to another, and pray one for another, that ye may be healed"* (James 5:15, emphasis mine). If the body of Christ was not so judgmental, more people would repent and confess their sins to others so they can be delivered. Are we more interested in exposing their transgression or attempting to rescue them from their error or bondage? James goes on to say, *"Brethren, if any of you do err from the truth, and one convert him; Let him know, that he which converteth the sinner from the error of his way shall save a soul from death, and shall hide a multitude of sins"* (19, 20).

I am not giving a license for an individual to sin. If a person does not repent, then their sin needs to be exposed. Paul the apostle wrote to the Corinth church and exposed a man who was committing adultery with his father's wife (step-mother). (Sounds like the contemporary soap opera, *Days of Our Lives.*) At the time of Paul's writing, the man was not willing to repent so Paul said, "Put him out of the church." But some time later the same man repents, so in 2 Corinthians, therefore, Paul invited him back into fellowship with the saints. Paul did not invite him back with stipulations or demands. He was invited to come back as if it did not ever happen.

The only Bible someone may every see is you or me.

Jesus made it clear; if someone claims to be a disciple, if they claim to have His spiritual DNA and possess *the Galilean Gene*, then that individual must love as He loved. What is the evidence of Discipleship?—it is love. The Bible tells us, *"We know that we have passed from death unto life, because we love the brethren. He that loveth not his brother abideth in death"* (1 John 3:14). Love is a mandate in scripture. The proof of Discipleship is love. *"Beloved, let us love one another; for love is of God; and every one that loveth is born of God, and knoweth God"* (1 John 4:7).

This quality is not an option. We cannot claim to be a disciple if we do not replicate the character of Christ. John also said, *"Whosoever doeth not righteousness is not of God, neither he that loveth not his brother"* (1 John 3:10b). The genetic code for Discipleship is love. It is the foundational support to identify ourselves with Christ. To say we can be a disciple and not show compassion, mercy or kindness to others is a trap of the devil. For *"If a man say, I love God, and hateth his brother, he is a* LIAR" (1 John 4:20, emphasis mine).

When an infant is born, it is common for others to comment, "He or she looks like their mother/father." The feature of a child comes from his or her parents. When others look at us, who do they say we look like? Jesus said, *"By this shall all men know that ye are my disciples, if ye have love one to another."* Do we carry the *Galilean Gene*? Do our actions reflect the identity of Jesus? The Prominent gene— love—is the key!

The Bible says,

> *"Love is patient and kind. Love is not jealous or boastful or proud 5 or rude. It does not demand its own way. It is not irritable, and it keeps no record of being wronged.6 It does not rejoice about injustice but rejoices whenever the truth wins out.7 Love never gives up, never loses faith, is always hopeful, and endures through every circumstance"* (1 Cor. 13:4-7, NLT).

If we are to have genes that fit, we need to discover the prominent gene—love. This distinguishing quality will cause others to notice we are a disciple. The first sign of God's DNA in a disciple is love. People should see us walk, hear us talk, and watch us act appropriately like our genealogical heritage. If we have the *Galilean Gene,* we will be mistaken for Jesus. The only Bible someone may every see is you or me. Can they see the prominent gene? If not, what will happen to them now?

8

_____

The Recessive Gene

What are genes? They are not the pants you put on to play in or wear to go somewhere. They are one of the many parts of the cells that make up all living things. We have established that genes are passed on from parents to their children and determine what color hair the child will have, whether he or she will be tall or short, what color of eyes, and everything else about how the child looks. Genes are found on the chromosomes, inside the cells and contain the DNA codes for all the characteristics that humans and animals inherit.

There are two types of genes. The two types of genes are *dominant* and *recessive* genes. Dominant genes contain the characteristics that are the strongest and recessive genes contain the weaker characteristics. Examples of dominant gene characteristics are brown eyes and black fur or hair. (I will discuss further the dominant gene in the next chapter). Examples of recessive gene characteristics are blue eyes and gray or red fur. If one parent passes on a dominant gene, the offspring will have that dominant color. For a recessive color to show up in the offspring, both parents must pass on recessive genes for the same fur color. For example, if one parent passes on a gene for brown eyes and the other passes on a gene for blue eyes, the offspring will have the brown eyes, as it is the dominant gene. The offspring would only have the blue eyes if both parents passed on the recessive gene for blue eyes.[1]

Genes simplistically do their work by making a protein. Each gene has a double copy - one from the mom one from the dad. If the protein from the mom is more effective at doing its job, it is dominant; and if the one from the dad is less effective, it is recessive.[2]

The effect of a recessive gene depends on the trait. Remember that DNA codes for traits and contains the instructions for making proteins. Proteins have many functions in the body: structural, hormones, other messenger type molecules, etc. A recessive trait may code for a protein that is either less functional or perhaps non-functional.3

In nonprofessional terms, the recessive gene is submissive to the dominant gene. The dominant gene is the greater (master) and the recessive is the lesser (servant). The only time a recessive gene will function appropriately is when two or more recessive genes correspond simultaneously. The byproduct of corresponding recessive genes is to produce a characteristic or feature that is intended to be the lower trait (humble).

The association of the dominant and recessive genes illustrates several key spiritual attributes. One of these divine traits is submission. Secondly, the recessive gene demonstrates a characteristic of servant hood that should manifest in a disciple. Thirdly, for descriptive purposes, when two recessive genes act similarly, they create a neutral gene or similar behavior. This is to reveal the willingness of a disciple to be humble in like manner of Christ. In other words, if the *Galilean Gene* was recessive in a particular area, the disciple should also be recessive in the same. Therefore, the two recessive genes (spiritually speaking) produce the same results. As Jesus submitted to the Father, we ought to follow His example. Jesus surrendered His will: so should we.

A Disciple is Recessive by Definition
The Bible is clear about the function of the recessive gene:

> *"The disciple is not above his master, nor the servant above his lord."*
>
> Matthew (10:24)

> *"The disciple is not above his master: but every one that is perfect shall be as his master."*
>
> (Luke 6:40)

> *"Verily, verily, I say unto you, The servant is not greater than his lord; neither he that is sent greater than he that sent him."*
>
> (John 13:16)

Throughout this book, I have attempted to define the word disciple. It has had varied definitions in each chapter. We have discovered diverse principles of God's DNA that are to appear in the disciple's genetic code. This chapter is no exception. The recessive gene is found in the very definition of the word disciple.

The term disciple is used consis-tently in the four Gospels to describe the relationship between Christ and His followers. Jesus used it when He was speaking to them and then employed it when referring to one another. The word disciple did not lose its significance after Christ completed His earthly ministry and returned to heaven. In fact, the word disciple is used in the entire book of Acts. To be a member of the Early Church, it was required to be a disciple of Jesus Christ. This is not to be mistaken for "church membership."

A disciple possesses the recessive gene.

The call of God and the demand of Christ still carries the same meaning. If we are to follow Him, it will take a deep commitment. We must be willing to sell out and give all to Him. The Early Church was willing to make this dedication and bear the title - disciples (Acts 1:15; 6:1; 2, 9; 9:1, 19; 25, 26, 38; 11:26, 29; 13:52; 14:20, 22, 28; 15:10; 18:23, 27; 19:1, 9, 30; 20:1, 7, 30; 21:4, 16). The term disciple was used to describe individuals in the Church before the term Christian was used. They were first called Christians at Antioch in Acts 11:26.

The term Christian meant something to the Early Church and throughout church history. But in North America, the word has become too common; it has lost its meaning and significance. Its original meaning identified a person with Christ, for in the Greek, "Christian" literally means, "little Christ's."

The term "disciple" in Greek literally means "one who sits under or sits at one's feet – like a pupil, student or a taught one." The idea carries the posture of the recessive gene. The position a follower would take when being taught by a Rabbi was to sit at his feet. In this case, the suggestion refers to the teacher, Christ and his under studies, or disciples. As a Master, the teacher was to impart knowledge to his learner. Jesus can impart all the purposes of God necessary to discover and fulfill His will. He is not merely a lecturer in whose dissertations we may ascertain a few lessons. No, Jesus is more than that. Jesus attempted, literally, to pour Himself into His disciples so that they could identify with the *Galilean Gene* as much as His teaching. Therefore, you can look into the face of the student and see genes of the teacher.

Have you ever looked at an athlete and been able to identify his or her teacher or coach? If you listen closely to a singer or musician, you can often identify who influenced his or her. It is only natural that the student takes on the genetic character of the teacher. If you and I are going to be successful disciples, we must take on the characteristics of Jesus Christ. It is more than instruction it is a relationship. This relationship is the inherited Divine DNA.

Religion will eliminate relationship. To be a disciple, it takes more than a formal ceremony, liturgy, religious activity or having your name on a church membership role. To attend church does not make you a Christian. It takes a DNA transformation to obtain this type of identity.

According to the Scriptures, a disciple is not above his teacher or master. A disciple possesses the recessive gene in his very nature. The recessive gene bears a significance trait, which clearly defines a disciple.

Types of Recessive Genes

The recessive gene, spiritually speaking, is based upon the traits that were manifested in the life of Christ. The recessive gene (submission) that was in Jesus produced its function when He submitted to the Heavenly Father. In the previous chapter, we discussed the humility of Christ that was involved as He became a human. In this chapter, we shall review the specific recessive genes that were in Jesus and are thus inherited by the disciple.

The *Galilean Gene* carries both dominant and recessive genes. Whenever the recessive gene corresponded with the will of the Father (dominant), the recessive gene surrendered. This attribute has been genetically passed on to the disciple. Therefore, when we see a recessive trait in Jesus, we will automatically see a recessive gene in the disciple's DNA. We have inherited the gene. We are different by design. The corresponding results are recessive in nature. It produces the same byproduct—a surrendering spirit.

There are four recessive genes found in the *Galilean Gene*; submission, suffering, sympathy and service. These four recessive genes have been genetically passed to His disciples. These recessive genes are part of the disciple's DNA and are to function the way they were inherited. These four genes are to be the indicators that will determine the DNA code for a disciple.

Recessive-Submission Gene

Biblical *submission* is "not" synonymous with blind obedience! God's Word uses two distinctive Greek words, one for *obedience* and another for *submission*, when referring to the function of various subordinates within governing establishments. The Greek word "Hupakouo" is normally used in Scripture for obedience.4 Its technical meaning is "under the hearing of commands." A Biblical command for obedience is often followed by a promise of blessing to the subject who complies or with a warning of negative consequences to the subject who chooses noncompliance.

Under the command for obedience, the subordinate is offered no alternative but to obey, nor is he allowed to debate the question of whether he should or should not obey. The appointed authority enforces compliance, executes judgment and stands responsible for the results of his rule. The only responsibility of the subject under obedience is to do what he is told.

An example of the concept of obedience (as opposed to submission) is found in Colossians 3:22-25. Christian slaves were instructed to remain obedient to their masters and to serve wholeheartedly, as if they were serving the Lord Himself. In Ephesians 6:1-3, God commands children to obey their parents.

The most imperative directive for obedience is an individual's response to Jesus Christ as savior. The Bible says, *"And to you who are troubled, rest with us, when the Lord Jesus shall be revealed from heaven with his mighty angels, In flaming fire taking vengeance on them that know not God, and that obey not the gospel of our Lord Jesus Christ; Who shall be punished with everlasting destruction from the presence of the Lord, and from the glory of His power"* (I Thessalonians 1:7-9).

Obedience to the Gospel of Jesus Christ refers to the personal acceptance of Christ as the only way to eternal salvation. This example warns that the consequences for disobedience (that is, non-acceptance of Christ as Savior) will be everlasting separation from the presence and power of the Lord.

The second Greek word used in the Bible when referring to the function of subordinates is "Hupotasso" which means, "to yield, submission".5 Technically, submission means "under placement or position, status or rank." This word is used by the writers of Scripture to refer to the positions and attitudes of subjects under the authority of their government (I Peter 2:13-15), to believers under the teaching authority of their pastors (Hebrews 13:17), and of wives under the leadership of their husbands (Ephesians 5:22). The Biblical definition of submission includes the willing and positive response of a subordinate to his rightful authority. The submissive subject "consciously and freely yields" his or her own will to the will of the authority.

An example of Biblical submission is Christ's submission to God the Father in the Garden of Gethsemane just prior to His death on the cross. Christ's example reveals that submission is not an act of blind obedience; but instead, it is a conscious act of a subordinate choosing to yield his will to the will of his authority. *"And he was withdrawn from them about a stone's cast, and kneeled down, and prayed, Saying, Father, if thou be willing, remove this cup from me; nevertheless, not my will, but thine, be done"* (Luke 22:41-42).

Ephesians 5:21 (NLT) - *"And further, you will submit to one another out of reverence for Christ"*, is to be regarded as every soul to be subject to higher powers. *"For there is no power but of God: the powers that be are ordained of God... Render therefore to all their dues: tribute to whom tribute, custom to whom custom, fear to whom fear, honour to whom honour"* (Rom. 13:1, 7).

"Obey them that have the rule over you, and submit yourselves, for they watch for your souls, that they may give account, that they may do it with joy and not with grief" (Heb. 13:17).

"Fear God, honour the king" (1 Pet. 2:17).

The recessive gene is a feature appointed by God, which we are required to observe. This is true of *ecclesiastical power.* God has ordained that there shall be teachers and they taught - governors and they governed. He raises up those who are to have the supervision of others, and those under the supervisors are required to subordinate themselves to their authority (Heb. 13:17). But their rule is administrative and not legislative, directive more than authoritative, and managed by a godly council rather than a court.

Here too there must be *mutual* submission, for in both governors and governed there is mutual service. The governors themselves are but "ministers" (1 Cor. 4:1). They have indeed an honorable office, yet they are only *servants* (2 Cor. 4:5), whose work is to feed the flock, to act as directors or guides by word and example (1 Tim. 4:12). Though they *"are over you in the Lord"* (1 Thess. 5:12), yet not *"as being lords over God's heritage"* (1 Pet. 5:5) but as motivated by love for souls, seeking their edification, gently endeavoring to persuade rather than dominate them.

The governing principle of the recessive-submission gene is to willingly yield to the will of the Father. The disciple inherits the *Galilean Gene*; therefore, God's DNA imparts a recessive trait called submission.

Recessive-Suffering Gene

The second identifying trait for a recessive gene is *suffering*. The source of this suffering is persecution from without. *"And ye shall be hated of all men for my name's sake: but he that endureth to the end shall be saved"* (Matthew 10:22). Jesus was explaining that if a follower looks like, talks like and acts like Him, bearing His characteristics—because the world hated Him, they will naturally hate the disciple.

It seems like today's Christians have the tendency to seek after the accolades of men and want to be accepted by the world. *If we are true disciples, what we stand for in our life is diabolically opposed to the world.* What the world says is right - Scripture says it is wrong.

The concept of persecution is unfamiliar to the US, but in other parts of the world, it is common. In Red China, if it is discovered that you are a disciple, you will be arrested and committed to prison. If you are a preacher, you can lose your life. In India, they tie Christians to a tree and skin them alive. In various parts of North Africa, they sell Christians into slavery; and in Sudan, they dismember their body parts to "mark" them as Christians.

What if you got was coming to you?

However, in America, we are under social prejudices and political persecution. It appears that the liberals and the ACLU accept religious freedom, but not for Christians. They have removed prayer from public schools, the name of God from courtrooms and removed special annual Christian events from holidays.

To be a Christians, we must realize *suffering* is inevitable and it is a recessive trait. Paul said, *"That I may know him, and the power of his resurrection, and the fellowship of his sufferings, being made conformable unto his death"* (Philippians 3:10). If the world rejected Him, it will reject you and me.

We will not only suffer persecution from without but from within. Jesus said, *"It is enough for the disciple that he be as his master, and the servant as his lord. If they have called the master of the house Beelzebub, how much more shall they call them of his household?"* (Matthew 10:25). People of your own household will oppose you. Jesus had the elders of Israel, the scribes, the Pharisees, the Sadducees and members of the Sanhedrin say His method of ministry was of Satan. The Son of God was accused of being a devil. If religion called Jesus a devil, how much more will they accuse His disciples of the same?

Even the family members of Jesus challenged His authenticity. If you are radical for Christ, someone at sometime will question your motive and intentions. Do not be surprised if people in church or your own family bring you opposition. When you are about to step up and go to another level with God, someone will come against you. Others will criticize you at work, run your name down, and talk negatively about you with the attempt to slander your stand for Christ.

Therefore, if you are not suffering any kind of persecution, one of two things is pending. One, you have not been saved long enough; do not worry, suffering will visit you eventually. Two, if you do not experience any difficulty or opposition, are you really a disciple?

When I was nineteen and new to ministry, I had already preached a number of times. An older minister came up to me, and asked, in reference to the ministry, "How is it going?" I replied, "Well, I don't know. How can you tell if it is going all right?" He spoke up and declared, "Well, two things you can count on, people are getting saved and people are getting mad." I responded,

"Well, both of those things are happening so I must be doing pretty well." This was true for Jesus. When He preached the Gospel, some were saved and others were mad. Opposition and suffering is an indicator that you are a disciple of Christ.

Opposition was evident against the Church in the 1800's. When persecution was at its height, on a dark December evening, while sitting on the couch, the wife of Charles Spurgeon, the prince of preachers, said, "I felt the darkness penetrate my soul, how can I go on?" She began to pray to God for help, asking for relief from the heaviness of ministry, when she heard a soft whistling noise in the room. It was winter and nighttime so she knew it could not be a bird outside making the noise. She followed the sound and realized it was coming from the fireplace in the room. A hole in a piece of oak was sending a certain pitch from the flames. Then suddenly, God spoke to her, "I created that tree and placed it there to create the unique sound for you to hear. Nevertheless, had it not been for the fire you would never have heard it." We want the world to hear the sound of the Gospel, but they will never experience it until we go through the fire of trial.

That which is in us may never come out until we are in the fire. Shadrach, Meshach, and Abednego released a revival in Nebuchadnezzar's day when they were willing to go into the fire. When the fire was seven times hotter than normal, God could have kept and spared them, but He allowed them to be cast into the furnace. God could have extinguished the flames, but He decided to do something greater. Had God chosen to prevent this event, their testimony would not have carried the miraculous impact. They did not proclaim how God delivered them from it, but how He delivered them through it. The king would have never seen the fourth man (the Son of God) in the fire had they been averted from the persecution. The world had a revelation of Jesus when His disciples were put in the fire. Their suffering created their opportunity to testify.

Did you know that Paul the Apostle wrote more than half of the New Testament? But before he was Paul he was called Saul of Tarsus. He was converted while traveling to Damascus, attempting to arrest Christians and persecuting them for their faith. Saul held the garments when the Pharisees stoned Stephen. While stones were blasting against Stephen's body, it was then he declared, *"I see Jesus, standing at the right hand of the Father"* (Acts 7:59). Notice that when other references refer to Jesus and the right hand of the Father, it says He was sitting at the right hand. In this story, He was standing. What made Jesus stand that day? It was when one of His disciples was willing to endure suffering and persecution. Jesus said, "Those who endure to the end shall be saved" (Matt. 10:22).

When God confronted Saul He asked him, "Why do you kick against the pricks?" Saul was persecuting Christians and opposing Jesus. However, it was through the suffering of Stephen, he saw the demonstration of Christ. Stephen's final words were, *"Forgive them for they know not what they do."* Does that sound familiar? It should - it was one of Jesus' final statements made from the cross at Calvary. Through identification, Stephen's suffering revealed Jesus to the man who would pen more than half of the New Testament and become the greatest missionary in the First Century.

The recessive-suffering gene is a trait that a disciple spiritually inherits. If we live a godly life, we will inadvertently provoke persecution. We do not need to be obnoxious, overbearing or haughty to incite persecution. It will come instinctively because we are diametrically opposed to the standards of this world. Jesus went against the "grain" of society, man's opinion, religion and governmental officials who opposed God's will. America may not inflame persecution to the level of Third World countries; but if we are a recessive gene carrier, we will collide with the secular humanist, feminist, gay activist, liberals, atheists, cults, false religions and Satanists. The spirit of this world is at work, and we shall suffer persecution for carrying the *Galilean Gene*. We may endure hardships for barring the recessive-suffering gene, but it will not prevent us from living a successful and abundant life (John 10:10). Jesus said, *"These things I have spoken unto you, that in me ye might have peace. In the world ye shall have tribulation: but be of good cheer; I have overcome the world"* (John 16:33).

Recessive-Sympathy Gene

The third trait that identifies us with the recessive gene is *sympathy*. Jesus said,

> *"But love ye your enemies, and do good, and lend, hoping for nothing again; and your reward shall be great, and ye shall be the children of the Highest: for he is kind unto the unthankful and to the evil. Be ye therefore merciful, as your Father also is merciful. Judge not, and ye shall not be judged: condemn not, and ye shall not be condemned: forgive, and ye shall be forgiven: Give, and it shall be given unto you; good measure, pressed down, and shaken together, and running over, shall men give into your bosom. For with the same measure that ye mete withal it shall be measured to you again."* (Luke 6:35-38).

Likewise, we ought to be people of sympathy, love, mercy, graciousness and giving. A disciple of Jesus bears His characteristics. He did not judge. He did not look down on those who were hurting. He showed mercy. In our own identity, we are naturally bent toward judgment. It is an "eye for eye" mentality. We think, "What goes around comes around" or "Their day's coming." I have seen individuals actually get upset when someone they were mad at was saved, because God would not judge that person for how someone wronged them. At that point, they can no longer be angry with them and it was God's fault. What if you got what was coming to you?

It is too easy to look down on the man in the gutter, with his hands wrapped around the brown paper bag disguising his alcohol bottle. Do we walk by as if he is less than a dog? Are we too quick to judge a homeless person, a drug addict or one with a perverse mind? If it were not for the mercy of God, it would be you or me in the alley, on the street or in rehab.

America receives most of its trends and sociological norms from the UK. Hairstyles, fashion and ethical mindsets slip across the Atlantic. According to the BBC in the United Kingdom, a survey said, "Twice as many people would feel sympathy for a homeless dog than for a homeless person with drug or mental health problems." Some 2,000 people across the UK were questioned for the survey and 41% of those questioned believed many homeless people did not want to be housed, the BBC survey found that.6

The foundation of a growing church is humility.

How many times should we reach out to a person who has failed, fallen or sinned? How many times should we show mercy to the downcast? How many times should we offer sympathy? Every time? Yes, every time they need it! Jesus said,

> *"For I was an hungred, and ye gave me no meat: I was thirsty, and ye gave me no drink: I was a stranger, and ye took me not in: naked, and ye clothed me not: sick, and in prison, and ye visited me not. Then shall they also answer him, saying, Lord, when saw we thee an hungred, or athirst, or a stranger, or naked, or sick, or in prison, and did not minister unto thee? Then shall he answer them, saying, Verily I say unto you, Inasmuch as ye did it not to one of the least of these, ye did it not to me"* (Matthew 25:43-45).

The disciple of Jesus should refrain from prejudice, discrimination, injustice and bigotry. We cannot be His disciple and hate someone because of his or her gender, race, creed, color or nationality. We cannot be His disciple if we do not take on his characteristics. God sent His Son into the world to die for a sinner. That was love. God does not hate anyone and neither should we.

When Peter had a vision of a sheet with a variety of animals, God was confronting his prejudices against the Gentiles. The Lord declared, "What I have called clean, who are you to call it unclean?" If God could look at an uncircumcised Gentile and see him saved, so must Peter. After he obtained the understanding, he went to Cornelius' house and the Gentile Pentecost broke out.

Is it possible that the Church has grown cold to society's problems and we sit comfortably in our pews to the point that the helpless, hopeless, and homeless are crying out and we cannot hear them? I realize that certain churches may have a particular calling to their community or a certain attribute in the overall body, but every disciple should inherit the recessive-sympathy gene, which would cause them to react according to the *Galilean Gene*. Here the words of Jesus again, *"Inasmuch as ye did it not to one of the least of these, ye did it not to me"* (Matt. 25:45). Sympathy should be an instinctive reaction because it is in our genes.

Recessive-Service Gene

The fourth trait that identifies us with a recessive gene is *service*. When Jesus was in the Upper Room with the Twelve, an argument broke out. They were debating who would be the greatest in the Kingdom. Luke says, *"And there was also a strife among them, which of them should be accounted the greatest"* (22:24). What is so amazing about the timing of this dispute is that it transpired immediately after Jesus washed their feet—a sign of humility and service. Jesus took on the role of the lowest of servants that was assigned to wash visitors' feet when they entered their master's home.

In the middle of the Passover meal, Jesus leaves the table, takes a towel and a basin of water, and then begins to remove the disciple's sandals. Once they realized what He was doing, they began to protest his actions. In fact, Peter refused to allow Jesus to administer foot washing. It was not because of the act, but because the position or role Jesus was imitating. Peter was mortified because he was sitting above Jesus. It was in this context Jesus said, *"If I wash thee not, thou hast no part of me"* (John 13:8).

It is just as vital to understand the role of an individual as to take on the role of one who is your mentor. It was bad enough that Jesus was humbling Himself, but if he allowed Jesus to follow through, then he would later have to wash the feet of someone who was lower than he was. Peter and the other disciples were arguing among themselves to discover who was the greatest.

It is all too easy to be selective with the characteristics of Christ, attempting to eliminate certain passages of Scripture to avoid unpleasant situations and people. Do we make excuses for our behavior attempting to circumvent responsibility? It is excessively common to hear someone say, "But, you do not know what they did to me" or "You have to understand; that is just the way I was raised." If we are not willing to humble ourselves to a place of servant hood, we miss the meaning of discipleship.

We live in a society of selfishness, consumed with wants, and willing to help someone else ONLY if it benefits us! Adults in the church are behaving like children in a grown world and preventing the spread of the Gospel. It takes a DNA reformation of heart to operate with a recessive-service gene. Jesus humbled Himself and was willing to die for humanity. His attitude was, "I did not come into the world to be served, but to serve."

What would happen in the church if we could eliminate a "greater than thou" attitude? The "hierarchy mentality" thinks that they are so vital to the success of the church that if they were not involved, it would not get accomplished. I had a person say to me once, "I am thinking about leaving this church; and if I do, what will you do without me?" Friend, no one is indispensable. With this attitude, the church might be better off without you! Do we actually think that a church would collapse without us? No, Jesus said, *"Upon on this rock, I will build my church."* That is a promise. The foundation of a growing church is servant hood.

I was preaching in a Camp Meeting with a man named Andy Miller, who, at that time, was the commissioner with the Salvation Army. He is a great man and one of the greatest preachers I have been privileged to know. He told a story one night at this meeting and I would like to share it with you. One of the first churches he pastored was in the suburbs of a large city. A man named Willie was saved under Andy's ministry. Before his conversion, Willie was an average person, uneducated and rough around the edges from his upbringing on the streets. With a basic job, he lived in a humble home.

On one occasion, Willie approached Andy and discussed how when he was young he would watch the Salvation Army march in parades. He said he was overwhelmed with their demeanor, their uniforms and posture. He asked Andy if it was possible for him to receive the honor of wearing a uniform and doing work for the church. Andy was blessed to hear this; but at the time, Willie was lacking in personal hygiene. Therefore, he consented but with this condition: Willie had to keep the Salvation Army suit clean and pressed, with shined shoes, and wear it with pride. However, if Willie did not keep his end of this bargain, the suit would be retracted. Willie, with glee and excitement, said he would keep it clean as promised.

One fall evening, the temperature was extremely low and Willie knew of some widows who would need wood for heat. Therefore, all night long, he chopped wood and carried it to the porches of these unfortunate widows. He finished around four o'clock in the morning. When morning came, he did not have time to clean his suit, so he headed out to church. Andy was already at the pulpit as Willie entered the church. He could see his uniform was filthy with dirt and mud.

When the service ended, Andy pulled Willie aside and confronted him due to his dirty uniform. He informed Willie he was going to have to take back the suit. Willie begged him not to take the suit. Andy reminded him of the deal. Willie explained how the unexpected frost caused some of the widows in the community to go without heat and how he chopped wood all night. Tears running down Willie's face, he described how he would do better in the future to keep the suit clean. He said he was sorry and that he was just trying to help those who were in need. He begged Andy not to take his suit.

Andy said, about that time the Holy Spirit began to speak to him. Suddenly, Andy was humbled because he was more interested in a clean suit than serving. It was as if he had forgotten the purpose and mission of the Salvation Army. Andy said he reached over to Willie, removing the wood chips and dirt, and began rubbing them on his uniform. He continued until he had removed most of the debris from Willie's suit and then wrapped his arms around him. As Andy embraced him with humility, he said, "Forgive me, Willie. Don't worry about the suit. We can get it cleaned." Andy was reminded what the purpose of the uniform was - service.

Jesus came to the earth to touch people who are lost and hopelessly hurting. Not everyone who cries, "Lord, Lord" will enter the Kingdom. Those who do the will of God will be welcomed in that day. He will say to others, "Depart from me I never knew you." A recessive gene is in every disciple, but do we know it? Discipleship is being identified with Jesus. It is having a deep relationship with Him. The *Galilean Gene* has the recessive gene trait and it is passed down to God's disciples. If we have God's DNA, we have the recessive gene and it will produce the same traits inside of us. We carry the recessive-submission, suffering, sympathy and service gene. Be careful, this gene is contagious!

9

The Dominant Gene

I n the last chapter, we discovered the purpose of recessive genes and their correlation to dominant genes. Let us review to familiarize ourselves with this gene. The dominant gene is a trait that will appear in the offspring if one of the parents contributes it. It is called dominant because it overrides the recessive gene.

In humans, dark hair is a dominant trait; if one parent contributes a gene for dark hair and the other contributes a gene for light hair, the child will have dark hair.

An example is the gene for blossom color in many species of flowers—a single gene controls the color of the petals, but there may be several different versions (or *alleles*) of the gene. One version might result in red petals, while another might result in white petals. The resulting color of an individual flower will depend on which two alleles it possesses for the gene and how the two interact.

Strictly speaking, genes are not dominant or recessive; only alleles are. The word allele comes from the Greek word, αλληλος, meaning "each other."[1] An allele (pronounced al-eel or al-e-ul) is any one of a number of viable DNA coding that occupies a given *locus* (position) on a chromosome. Alleles are DNA (deoxyribonucleic acid) sequences that make up the code for a gene. An individual's *genotype* for that gene is the set of alleles it happens to possess. A genotype is the composition of part of an individual's hereditary information, which contributes to determining a specific trait.

A dominant gene is the contributing trait that enables us to express the *Galilean Gene*. It is what makes us disciples. Without this gene, we would be ineffective, helpless and incapable of fulfilling its design. The dominant gene is the spiritual DNA that identifies us with Christ. This gene gives us the ability to live like HIM. Our *Divine by Design* DNA is the source that drives us. In fact, it is what makes us look like our Father and act like Jesus.

The dominant gene in a believer is the inherited parental characteristic that defines our behavior. It is the most important, effective or significant trait that identifies a disciple. It is as necessary as the air we breathe and the water we drink. It is our resource!

Daddy's Dominant Gene

The important factor to remember is that the dominant gene is the parental DNA that controls the spiritual genetic make-up for a disciple. This type of gene comes from the Holy Spirit, who passes God's DNA. A dominant trait that was in Jesus is deposited into us. *"The Spirit of God, who raised Jesus from the dead, lives in you. And just as he raised Christ from the dead, he will give life to your mortal body by this same Spirit living within you"* (Rom. 8:11, NLT). We have our Daddy's DNA.

The deposit of the dominant gene was so important that just prior to Jesus' departure after His post-resurrection appearances, He reminded His followers to expect a DNA transformation. The dominant gene was not to be excluded; it was reinforced by a PROMISE! Jesus told them to remain in Jerusalem and to *"Wait for the promise of the Father, which, saith he, ye have heard of me. For John truly baptized with water; but ye shall be baptized with the Holy Ghost not many days hence"* (Acts 1:4, 5, emphasis mine).

This promise of the Father was not just for the 120 believers on Pentecost. Every believer is a candidate! The genetic transfer delivers God's DNA, and it possesses a dominant gene. Jesus described the dominant trait as *fire*. In order for individuals to go further with God, they must receive a baptism and allow the fire to ignite the dominant gene. By comparing it to John's baptism, fire was a *resource* that was to accompany the baptism of the Holy Ghost.

We may have several dominant genes. However, I would like to expound upon three of them that Jesus said would mark us and cause us to make a difference in the world. These dominant genes can change our lives, family, community, nation and the world. The three dominant genes are *power*, *identity* and *witness* genes. They will mark us as a child of God. When these three genes activate there is no question, "Whose kid we are." We cannot help it. We look like our Daddy; we can call Him, *Abba* (Rom. 8:15).

Dominant Gene: Power

The first dominant gene is power. *"But ye shall receive power, after that the Holy Ghost is come upon you: and ye shall be witnesses"* (Acts 1:8a, emphasis mine). Jesus said, *"Ye shall receive POWER."* The word for power in Greek is *dunamis*. Our English word, dynamite comes from dunamis, which means might or strength.

When was the last time you went to church and said, "It was dynamite"? Our corporate worship encounters ought to be explosive. The book of Acts describes how the Early Church operated in power. Religion, scholars, and theologians have tried to place a title on this experience. Some have called it regeneration - others, sanctification; some call it "filled with the Holy Ghost" and then some, "Baptized in fire."

Do we know who we are?

Regardless of what we title the power encounter, it is important that we experience it. Now, if we say we have what they inherited at Pentecost, then why do we not DO what they DID? If we have this *dominant-power gene*, we will do the same thing as they did as in the book of Acts. How can we believe we can receive the same power and then think we cannot do the same thing they did? God is no respecter of persons! His dominant gene is transferred to His children.

In Acts chapter three, Peter and John met a crippled man at the gate Beautiful. He was begging for money. Peter said, *"Silver and gold have I none; but such as I have give I thee: IN the name of Jesus Christ of Nazareth rise up and walk"* (3:6). We have programs, multiple staff members, microphones, nice buildings and money—but do we have the power? Peter said, *"Such as I have give I thee."* If we do not have it, we cannot give it.

We may have pretty preaching, marvelous music and terrific talent, but none of this will save anybody. However, if we possess all these qualities and combine them with the power and anointing of the Holy Ghost—we will touch everyone! There is preaching and then there is anointed preaching. Anointed preaching got 3,000 saved in their first meeting (Acts 2:41). If we allow the power to move in our lives, we can accomplish what HE wills!

Peter went and preached again. This time, 5,000 are saved (Acts 4:4). It caused a stir. The religious leaders asked, *"By what power, or by what name, have ye done this?"* (4:7). The Bible reveals the dominant gene in Peter for it says, *"Then Peter, filled with Holy Ghost, said unto them."* (4:8). Peter was full of God. The dominant-power gene was evident in him. When we are full of God, we can do the same works as the apostles. Peter told them, *"It is by the name of Jesus Christ of Nazareth, whom you crucified, whom God raised from the dead, even by him doth this man stand here before you whole"* (4:10). Peter believed that if he used Jesus' name, the power of the Holy Ghost would manifest.

We can use the name of Jesus and still have no power. If we were to go to certain churches today, we would see them use the name of Jesus. However, no one is being saved, healed or delivered. Where is the power? Disciples inherit the dominant-power gene from their Daddy. What is wrong with this picture?

The New Testament believers were a walking incarnation of spiritual energy. The dominant-power gene brought life-changing influence that verified the *Galilean Gene* was still eminent. Large crowds returned to see and hear a message that was accompanied by results!

It seems, nowadays, we cannot get people to shout in today's churches unless a cheerleader directs them. There is a lack of enthusiasm because there is a lack of power. The Early Church began in power and moved in power, but the Twentieth Century church has "dug into safety." It appears that we have huddled around Sunday school programs, song feasts, special meetings, revivals (which are necessary), but have hidden behind excuses and just tell stories of how it "used to be" in the good old days when God moved.

It is as if we have tried to store up the precious memories of the past and the moves of God in a box; and from time to time, we open it to remember what it was like before now. While the Israelites wandered in the desert, God provided manna. The miraculous provision was provided each morning. However, they became weary, going out each day to gather the heavenly supply. They decided to create a system where they could store up their blessing for a rainy day. But when they accumulated the manna it *"bred worms and stank"* (Exod. 16:20). Therefore, we have mannaism, scholasticism, institutionalism - all indicative of the absence of spiritual power. Do not get me wrong, I want to go to church. However, if the experience does not change my life, I am not going to go THERE!

Dominant Gene: Identity

One of the greatest problems I see in the body of Christ is the inability of people to know who they are in Christ. To understand the distinctive qualities we have inherited remains a mystery to many believers. Jesus knew who He was. He stated it many times in many ways. Nevertheless, do we know who we are? Pressures, problems, peril and perplexity of life have dominated people far too long! The stresses of living and dysfunctional homes have caused many believers to have low self-esteem, no self-confidence, insecurity and a poor self-image. If you are a disciple, let me tell you something—these "genes don't fit".

In order for us to live a life full of God, we must know who we are! *Identity* is a set of characteristics that somebody recognizes as belonging uniquely to himself or herself and constituting his or her individual personality for life. The *Galilean Gene* carries this *dominant-identity gene*, which identifies the disciple with his or her purpose and guides him or her to discover his or her destiny. Jesus was clear when He was attempting to encourage His followers before His death. He said, *"And I will ask the Father, and he will give you another Counselor, who will never leave you"* (John 14:16, NLT). This deals with insecurity, fear and feelings of abandonment. He continued saying, *"He is the Holy Spirit, who leads into all truth"* (John 14:17a, NLT). As long as Jesus was with them, He could only be at one place at one time. He was limited. However, the Holy Spirit does not have a physical body; therefore, He could live inside of all of them and go with them no matter where their physical geographical location took them. The Holy Spirit brings God's DNA. (I will discuss this further in the Conclusion).

Jesus reassured their doubts when He said, *"I am leaving you with a gift—peace of mind and heart. And the peace I give isn't like the peace the world gives. So don't be troubled or afraid"* (John 14:27, NLT).

The second emphasis in Acts 1:8 comes from the portion of the verse which says, *"After that the Holy Ghost is come upon you* (God's DNA): *and Ye SHALL BE"* (insert and emphasis mine). Stop there! I must reemphasize this point. We inherit God's DNA the moment the Holy Spirit comes upon us! Our genetic transformation is the regeneration, accompanied by the *Galilean Gene*! Stay with me - It will make sense in just a second. Then, *"Ye shall be"*! It is vital we see the meaning behind this word.

It's not activity— it's a lifestyle!

The three English words, *"ye shall be"* is one Greek word (ἔσεσθε).1 It is the future tense of εἰμί,2 pronounced ā-me, as with the feminine name, Amy. The word εἰμί means, "to be or to exist."3 Now allow me to put it together interpretively based upon the Greek understanding, *"After you experience the power of God, which will come upon you, caused by the presence of the Holy Spirit, you will come into existence and 'BE', which is to identify with ME and know who you are!"* (The Ervin Translation). This is the great DNA exchange! When we inherit God's genes, we become who we are and possess IDENTITY!

This is what I call the dominant-identity gene. I am not trying to overemphasize the Greek language, but I must point something else out to you. Incidentally, I heard a preacher friend of mine say once that he knows a LITTLE Greek and a LITTLE Hebrew. One owns a delicatessen and the other a bagel shop. (Just kidding.) Personally, I just read a lot. Now let me get back to my point.

Jesus knew who He was. In His teachings, He called Himself the "I AM." The Greek word for "I" is εγω, pronounced ā-go. Years ago a commercial ran for Eggo waffles. It showed two small children grabbing an Eggo waffle popping out of the toaster, yelling, "Let go of my Eggo!!" The Greek word for "I" sounds like Eggo. If we combine the Greek word εγω (eggo), "I" with εἰμί (Amy), "to be" it translates, "I AM." Our Lord did not have an identity crisis. He is the Great I AM. The dominant-identity gene transfers the divine genotype, which we inherit from the Father.

The DNA transfer gives us purpose and we receive the dominant trait—"TO BE." We exist for a purpose. We have instant identity. Our identity is in the Divine DNA. We are the reflection of Jesus. We are the image of the Father. We operate with power through the Holy Ghost. This genetic alteration causes us TO BE.

Therefore, we must understand that we must first BE before we DO. Our actions will be vain attempts if we do not know who we are. Our identity defines our behavior according to the image inside us. To DO is works, actions, and activity. They are necessary and serve their purpose; however, what we DO is not important unless we BE. TO BE does not mean we are who we are because of what we DO, but because we know who we ARE. We are God's children. "It's not activity—it's a lifestyle!"

The old phrase from Shakespeare fits well here. Hamlet's line, "To be or not to be, that is the question."4 In other words, before we can witness we must BE. To BE is to exist with a purpose. To BE is to imitate the nature of Christ. To BE is to identify with our inherited gene. To BE is to act according to our Divine DNA structure. We will BE, naturally. (No pun intended).

When we BE, we will not have to work up the skill, experience or the nerve to witness. When we BE, it just shows up! We cannot help ourselves. It will come automatically. It is like Peter in Acts chapter four, when the religious leaders told him to stop preaching or teaching in the name of Jesus. *"But Peter and John answered and said unto them, Whether it be right in the sight of God to hearken unto you more than unto God, judge ye. For we cannot but speak the things which we have seen and heard"* (Acts 4:19, 20). It was not that Peter was trying to decide if he should listen to their threats. It was the fact that Peter could not help but speak about Jesus. It was not something he did—it was something he was.

How do you stop being who you are? How can you quit being a BE? It is like telling me not to act like an Ervin. My Dad did not sit down with me and teach me to BE an Ervin. My father never pulled me aside to say, "Now, son, today I want to teach you how to BE an Ervin. Here's how an Ervin smiles, walks and smirks." No, he did not teach me how to BE an Ervin—it came naturally. No one had to teach me something I inherited.

Have you ever caught yourself saying something like this, "When I grow up, I am not going to act like my parents?" Then when you get older, have kids, you end up acting just like them!

My father passed away before my kids were born. I used to think to myself, "Katie and Alex (my two children) will never know my dad." One day, when Katie was only three, she was discussing a topic with me. Kids are notorious for asking why and debating with their parents. After several minutes of answering Katie's questions, I realized I was arguing with and being interrogated by a three-year-old. I abruptly finished the conversation by clapping my hands together, and said, "I've had my say" and got up to walk off.

Just then, I had a mental flash back. I could see my dad in my mind, simulating the same scenario. My father used to finish a conversation, abruptly clap his hands and say, "I've had my say." I had just acted like my father. I acted that way because I am an Ervin.

To BE means we act like our Father. It is comes naturally because we have His DNA. It is not something we DO - it is what we BE!

Dominant Gene: Witness

One of the most confusing concepts for believers is the meaning, *"Ye shall be my witnesses."* There must be hundreds, if not thousands, of books on witnessing. There is the *Roman Road*, *The Four Spiritual Laws*, *Evangelism Explosion*, soul-winning tracks and the list goes on. The concept of witnessing must come from our understanding of *"Ye shall be."*

The topic of our conversations is predominantly based upon who we are, what we identify with, or what consumes us. If a person is consumed with the weather, sports, music or hunting—that is all they talk about. That is how it is with the *dominant-witness gene.* Our conversation is based upon who we are, what we are identified with and what consumes us.

The promise of the Father was to receive power. Power produces us to BE. To BE then identifies us with our *Galilean Gene.* We are witnesses based upon our identity and the power that flows from our Divine DNA. Therefore, to share the gospel is an extension of who we are. We cannot help but demonstrate our behavior. We act like our Father. It just happens!

We should not have to persuade believers to witness. It should just happen! It should be as normal as breathing. We should not have to think about it. It happens because of who we BE!

When it comes to being witnesses, there are two fallacies that predominantly transpire with many Christians. They are called LIFE and WORD. The first style of witnessing is based upon a person's lifestyle. People in this category place the emphasis upon living a moral life or being a good person. If you were to hear them testify in church, they would say something like this, "Well, I want to thank the Lord for saving me. I am living my life for Jesus. I want to be a light upon a hill. I don't say a whole lot. I let my life do all my talking."

I am not saying that we should not live a godly life. We should and the Bible instructs us to do so. But the premise behind this form of witnessing carries the idea that an individual does not share his or her faith or speak to others. Simply put, they just mind their own business. They feel that if they act righteous without speaking, others will know they are disciples. Really?

The second type of witnessing is what I call WORD emphasis. You can see this manner in an individual who comes to work with a black, ten-pound, leather King James Version Bible that they prop upon their desk where they are employed. When they talk, every third word is either, "Praise the Lord," "Hallelujah," or "Glory to God." I am not saying we should not be exuberant about our faith or honor God in public. However, if we repeat these phrases constantly - borderline obnoxious - we can go overboard. Many times, these types of individuals are quick to judge and speak inappropriately. They are notorious to declare, "You're going to Hell!" All the while, thinking they are witnessing. What can we say? Something is wrong.

Now let me make this comment; I do not agree with the definition of these two types of witnessing. However, I do agree with the methods of witnessing—LIFE and WORD. To BE a witness means the dominant gene will automatically show up in our LIFE and our WORD. To BE is to demonstrate naturally the Life-Word witness gene.

This dominant-witness gene most commonly shows up in new believers. If they are exposed to a religious person, they may, over time, change their style of witnessing. Religion tends to have a DO-nothing attitude; just attend church, be a good ole boy, and point out people that are reprobates.

A new Christian has obtained the DNA of God. When it gets in them, they often bring a large number of people to Christ. Because religion emphasizes a system without recognizing the dominant-identity gene, they seldom operate with the dominant-witness gene.

I heard a true story of a young man who was a strong Christian and he attended a major University. On one occasion, he shared his faith with a close friend. His friend was apprehensive at first, and then asked, "If I become a Christian, do I have to tell anyone?" The young man was concerned that he would reject Christ, and frankly, did not know what to say. So he innocently said, "No, you don't have to tell anyone to become a Christian." The young man led him to the Lord.

Immediately after praying the sinner's prayer, they separated and headed to their classes. The new convert walked out of his dorm and did not go more than fifty paces before he saw a friend walking to class. He stopped his buddy and said, "Hey, you're not gonna believe what just happened to me. I just prayed and asked Jesus to come into my life. But the guy who prayed with me told me I didn't have to tell anyone. Isn't that great?" He prayed with his friend on the sidewalk and he became a Christian as well.

He continued along the pathway and met another friend. He told him the same thing and prayed the sinner's prayer with his friend. He made it to his classroom with over two-hundred students. He boldly testified to the students and said, "And he told me that I didn't have to tell anyone" Is not that amazing? He was so excited that he did not have to tell anyone, but he told everyone.

You do not have to read the Bible very long until you come across an incident where Jesus did a miracle for someone. They encountered the *Galilean Gene*. Then Jesus would tell them, "Go and tell no one." Then they went and told everyone. <u>Now</u> we are commanded to tell others, and we tell no one. If someone, who was just saved can witness, how much more should it happen to us.

Because we come from these two polarized extremes, we are ineffective in witnessing. It is not an either-

or; it is a both-and. Witnessing should be natural because it is based upon who you ARE, not what you DO. When we are consumed with the *Galilean Gene*, a divine power operates in us. We respond according to our DNA and not our training. We witness naturally out of relationship. We cannot help it. No matter what, if someone is consumed with something, he or she cannot help but talk about it.

I knew a person who was an engineer. When you talked with him, he could not help but explain everything as an engineer. He could take two hours explaining how to fry an egg. Because he was an engineer, he would go into extensive detail to break it down. What made him do that? Engineering was so much a part of his life, he could not do it any other way. What is in our life shows up in our WORD.

You cannot help it. It is not a program – knocking on doors, handing out flyers or surveying the neighborhood. Have you ever tried to program something that cannot be programmed? I have preached the Gospel for 17 years, and I have seen it repeatedly. A new Christian, who is not familiar with witnessing techniques and does not know what the Roman Road plan is all about, is the most effective witness. It is amazing to me. Many new Christians do not even know John 3:16, but they bring people to Christ. They say something like, "I don't know that much about it but you have got to come to church." Others say, "I cannot explain it, but here's what happened to me."

How can they witness effectively, bringing so many to Christ, when they do not know how to do it? It is because they recognize the gene in them. Are we are trying to follow a system and not connect with our dominant-witness gene? God forbid. The DNA of God is Life and Word. It is all that we are.

I have explained what witnessing is not and that it operates in new Christians who have not been exposed to religion. However, what does it mean when Jesus said, *"Ye shall be MY witnesses?"* (Emphasis mine). Notice that the pronoun, "MY" is possessive. Alex (my son) is a lot like me – strong-willed and stubborn. His vocabulary is progressing daily. He is active, energetic and full of life. Nevertheless, when he gets his mind set on something, it is difficult to convince him otherwise. If someone takes something from him that he has already determined belongs to him, he does not take it so well. In fact, he has had a tendency to let you know of his displeasure. He does not know how to articulate the words, "It's MINE!" yet; he does not know how to say it in body language.

When something belongs to you, you have sole ownership. When Jesus spoke of witnesses, He claimed possession. He was saying, "It's Mine!" "MY witnesses" indicate that there is a connection between Jesus and HIS witnesses. In other words, if we belong to Him, we will witness like Him! His character comes through. Ownership is the legal right to something. With His ownership, we ought to respond according to His DNA. Actually, our DNA comes from God; therefore, it should be automatic— We agree to reply to His WILL.

How are we to respond then? If we are HIS witnesses, what kind of witness are we? The Greek word for witness is μάρτυς, where we get our English word martyr.5 In Classical Greek this word implied "denoting the confirmation of a fact or an event."6 However, Luke uses the word witness – first in his gospel (Lk. 24:48) and again in Acts 1:8 in context to the risen Lord. Therefore, Luke is not using the word witness for witnesses of facts, but specifically as witnesses of the resurrection. By this very qualification, the apostles were authorized ambassadors.7

Luke uses the word witnesses throughout the book of Acts and it takes on a two-fold meaning. First, the life of a witness is a pathway of rejection –Rejection from religion as was in the case of Stephen (Acts 7). As witnesses, they would be rejected by the world, its system and by society. Second, as witnesses they did not consider their life their own. If necessary, they were willing to die for what they believed in. It is commonly believed that, when a general persecution was raised against the Christians by Nero about A.D. 64, under pretence that they had set Rome on fire, both Paul and Peter then sealed the truth with their blood.

Tradition teaches that Peter was crucified with his head downward and Paul was beheaded, around A.D. 64 or 65.8

Being a witness begins with power, followed by the DNA transformation through the Holy Spirit, which leads us to our identity and then the sobering thought that a disciple is willing to die for his faith. The dominant gene is the primary trait of a disciple. It is the finality of the DNA transformation. The key to *Galilean Gene* is to BE HIS WITNESSES. If we are to BE a dominant-gene carrier, we will duplicate the characteristic of Christ. His genetic code is in us. God's blueprint is structured in our spiritual DNA. We will DO what we DO because of who we ARE. It is who we were intended to BE. To possess the *Galilean Gene* means we are conformed to His image. Our spiritually-inherited genotype determines our behavior. Therefore, our discipleship genes are code oriented, not habit-forming oriented. We cannot help it. It is who we are. We are *Disciples by Design!* We look like our Daddy.

As a son or daughter of the Most High, the power in us causes us to be effective, to endure change so we can alter the course of history in the people we will meet. Our influence in our community, family or relationships will be dependant upon our ability to activate the *Galilean Gene*. Our traditions alone cannot empower us to BE who we were destined to BE.

I thank God for my Christian heritage, but my understanding about witnessing is not based upon power to DO witnessing but to BE a witness. Follow Acts 1:8 and do what I did. Step out of the paradigm of religion. Discover the liberty of the dominant gene in the person of the Holy Spirit.

Our gifting and talents are not enough. We need God's DNA to infuse us with power from on high! Paul said it best:

> *"And I, brethren, when I came to you, came not with excellency of speech or of wisdom, declaring unto you the testimony of God. 2 For I determined not to know any thing among you, save*

Jesus Christ, and him crucified. 3 And I was with you in weakness, and in fear, and in much trembling. 4 And my speech and my preaching was not with enticing words of man's wisdom, but in demonstration of the Spirit and of power: 5 That your faith should not stand in the wisdom of men, but in the power of God" (1 Cor. 2:1-5).

The power of God enables us to brace our spiritual identity and to BE all that we can be. We are His witnesses by design according to the *Galilean Gene*!

The DNA Conclusion

We have discovered that generally, a gene refers to a stretch of DNA, which encodes a single protein. We inherit two copies of each gene, one from our mother and one from our father. Many genes have multiple variants, which influence a given trait, which is called a *phenotype*. The phenotype of an individual organism describes one of its traits or characteristics that is measurable and that is expressed in only a subset of the individuals within that population. In other words, the phenotype is the detail description in the DNA that makes you unique. Paul described the spiritual phenotype in a regenerated person in 2 Corinthians, *"Therefore if any man be in Christ, he is a new creature: old things are passed away; behold, all things are become new"* (5:17). The word "creature" can mean a new species that never existed before. There is no one on the planet like you. Just like our physical phenotype, our spiritual phenotype carries our spiritual DNA. This imparts our destiny and purpose that only we can fulfill. We are *disciples by design*.

I have established several analogies between DNA and the spiritual make-up of a disciple in this book. Spiritually speaking, we have a divine genetic code that determines WHO WE ARE. These distinguishing characteristics dictate behavior. In the previous chapters, we determined that *dominant* and *recessive genes* contain *divine alleles*, which make up the originality of our being. We are a byproduct of the *Galilean Gene*. The *God-like genotype* is the hereditary data that causes us to act like God. Jesus tried to describe this when he quoted Psalms 82:6, which says, *"I say, 'You are gods and children of the Most High"* (NLT).

The Jewish leaders were struggling with what to do with Jesus. His actions depicted a prophet, but they wanted to know if He was the Messiah (John 10:24). His answer was not based upon His claims, but upon His relationship with His Father. *"The Father and I are one"* (John 10:30,

NLT). That is, God the Son has the same DNA as God the Father. Jesus did not inherit His DNA. He was not created as a god as the Jehovah's Witnesses misinterpret. The Divine nature He possessed in His body on earth was the same spirit He had before He came into Mary's womb.

In John 10, Jesus is not saying He was *a god* but that He WAS GOD. The son-ship of Jesus is simply a picture of the submission of Christ and the relationship between the Godhead. By becoming a human, Jesus surrendered the use of certain portions of His divine attributes, thus He was dependent upon the Holy Spirit and yielded to the Father's will. The *Galilean Gene* is Jesus genotype. It is the quality of God in a man. We receive the same gene, but we inherit it from the Father. The genetic code is deposited like a SEED inside us through the Holy Spirit. The SEED is Christ. We inherit God's DNA by means of the atonement of Jesus. Therefore, we become little gods. I did not say that, God did. *"Jesus answered the, Is it not written in your law, I said, Ye are gods? If he called them gods, unto whom the word of God came, and the scripture cannot be broken; Say ye of him, whom the Father hath sanctified, and sent into the world, Thou blaphemest; because I said, I am the Son of God?"* (John 10:34-36).

The genetic code of Christ, the *Galilean Gene*, carries God's DNA. When an individual receives this divine transfer, he or she gains a God-like genotype, which in return verifies the hereditary traits necessary to be a disciple. Jesus said, *"But when he sends the Counselor as my representative—and by the Counselor I mean the Holy Spirit—he will teach you everything and will remind you of everything I myself have told you"* (John 14:26, NLT).

God is waiting for us to receive His genetic code and to tell others about this life-changing experience. Jesus said it best, *"But I will send you the Counselor—the Spirit of truth. He will come to you from the Father and will tell you all about me. And you must also tell others about me because you have been with me from the beginning"* (John 15:26, 27, NLT).

My goal was not to write a book but to change lives. The *Galilean Gene* is the byproduct of God's DNA. We must spread the good news. It is time to BE a *Disciple by Design!*

ENDNOTES

Chapter 1

[1] http://ww.accessexcellence.org/g/AE/AEPC/NICH/gene03.html

[2] *Dictionary of New Testament Theology*, Colin Brown, editor, (Grand Rapids, MI: Zondervan) © 1986, Vo. I, p. 522.

[3] *Commentary on the Old Testament*, Keil & Delitzsch, (Peabody, MA: Hendrickson Publishers) © 1989, Vol. I, pp. 100, 101.

Chapter 2

[1] http://www.sciencentral.com/articles/view.php3?type=article&article_id=218392598

Chapter 3

[1] *A Greek-English Lexicon of the New Testament and Other Early Christian Literature*, F.W. Gingrich and Fredrick Danker, (Chicago,IL:The University of Chicago Press), © 1979, p. 356.

[2] Ibid. pp. 854, 55.

[3] Sermon: *"On Self Denial"* by Charles Finney at Oberlin College, April 27, 1859.

[4] Sermon 48: *"Self-denial"* by John Wesley, Works of Wesley, Thomas Jackson, editor, 1872 edition.

[5] *The Dwelling Place of God*, A.W. Tozer, The Alliance Witness, Chapter 25.

Chapter 4

[1] http://www.safe-food.org/-issue/ge.html

[2] http://en.wikipedia.org/wike/Human_genetic_engineering

Chapter 5

[1] http://en.wikipedia.org/wiki/Genealogical_DNA_test

[2] *Works of Wesley*, by John Wesley, Sermon 128, *"Free Grace"*, 1872 edition.

[3] Ibid. Sermon 14.

[4] *The Gospel Truth*, Sermon vii, Charles G. Finney, Gospel Truth Ministries, © 1999, 2000.

Chapter 6

[1] http://apnews.myway.com/article/20070411/D8OEJ3VO2.html

144

[2]http://cnews.canoe.ca/CNEWS/World/2007/04/23/4114325-ap.html
[3]http://crime.about.com/b/a/191150.htm
[4]http://abclocal.go.com/kgo/story?section=nation_world &id=4303111

Chapter 7
[1] *Dictionary of New Testament Theology,* Colin Brown, editor, four volumes, (Grand Rapids Michigan: Zondervan), © 1986, pp. 538, 539.
[2] *Strong's Exhaustive Concordance,* (Grand Rapids, Michigan:Baker Book House) © 1982, *Greek Dictionary of the New Testament,* p. 55.

Chapter 8
[1] http://www.promotega.org/vsu05022/genes.htm
[2] http://www.newton.dep.anl.gov/askasci/mole00/mole 00158.htm
[3] Ibid.
[4] *Vine's Expository Dictionary of Old and New Testament Words,* Reference Library Edition, (Iowa Falls, Iowa: Word Bible Publishers, © 1971, New Testament Dictionary p. 124.
[5] Ibid. pp. 86, 87.
[6] http://news.bbc.co.uk/1/hi/uk/6185862.stm

Chapter 9
[1] *The Interlinear Greek – English New Testament,* (London:Samuel Bagster and Sons Limited) © 1960, p. 463.
[2] *The analytical Lexicon to the Greek New Testament,* William D. Mounce, (Grand Rapids, MI: Zondervan Publishing House), © 1993, p. 217.
[3] Ibid. p. 164.
[4] The Tragedy of Hamlet, Act 3, Scene 1.
[5] *Vine's,* New Testament Dictionary, p. 225.
[6] *Dictionary of New Testament Theology,* Colin Brown, editor, Vol. III, pg. 1038.
[7] Ibid. p. 1043, 1044.
[8] http://www.biblestudy.org/question/sauldie.html